Work with Meaning, Work with Joy

Bringing Your Spirit to Any Job

Pat McHenry Sullivan

SHEED & WARD

Lanham, Chicago, New York, Oxford

Published by Sheed & Ward
An Imprint of Rowman & Littlefield Publishers, Inc.

A Member of the Rowman & Littlefield Publishing Group, Inc.
4501 Forbes Boulevard, Suite 200
Lanham, MD 20706

P.O. Box 317
Oxford
OX2 9RU, UK

Distributed by National Book Network

Library of Congress Cataloging-in-Publication Data

Sullivan, Pat McHenry.
    Work with meaning, work with joy : bringing your spirit to any job /
    Pat McHenry Sullivan
        p.cm. – (Spirit at work series)
    Includes bibliographical references.
    ISBN 1-58051-117-1 (pbk.)
      1.   Work—Religious aspects—Christianity. I. Title. II. Series

BT738.5 .S85 2003
248.8'8—dc21

                                       20032075826

Printed in the United States of America

Dedicated to the memory of my father,
William Howard McHenry

More than anyone else,
you modeled for me integrity, purpose, and joy.
Through your stories, you kept alive the meaningful
work of your parents, whom I never got to know,
and my mother, whose life ended much too soon.

Thank you for many hugs and laughs,
for reading the plan for my master's project
and asking how you could help,
for teaching me to see creativity
as a call from God and a gift from God.

Thank you for choosing Mayo Magdalene Lee
to be your wife, our mother,
and for choosing Violet Stahr
to help us be a whole family again.

Thank you for living, working, learning, dreaming, loving
until the very last hour
of the very last day.

Contents

Introduction

Exploring a New World of Spirit at Work

On the one hand, there is what matters most to you: life and health; relationships; service and creativity; adventure; laughter. Time to pet the cats, watch a sunset, have a meal with people you love. God, or whatever name you use for the divine mystery of creation and beyond.

On the other hand, there is work and all that goes with it: training for work; getting to and from work. Working, whether you want to or not. Office politics, performance reviews, projections of all kinds; recuperating from work; getting ready for another day at work.

For most adults, work and all it entails fill half or more of our waking hours. Too often, the "hands" for meaning and work are at odds, as if the only way to earn a living is at the expense of that which makes life worth living and as if status or things bought with money from working can substitute for the loss of meaning and joy.

Matthew Fox, an Episcopal priest who wrote *The Reinvention of Work*[1] and other popular books about spirituality, believes that spirit is too often strained out of students in the name of education. This distorts our vision of what work can and ought to be.

Fox says:

Work is not something just humans do by the sweat of their brow. That tree outside is working. It is sucking up juice and sunshine, giving birth to fruits and flowers. We should quit sitting around feeling sorry for ourselves because we work and realize that every being in the universe works!

Galaxies are spinning, grasses are growing, fishes are swimming, the sun is rising or whatever else it does to give off energy all day. So, work is about giving off our energy, a gifting of what is inside of us to the rest of the community. It's a way of returning blessing for blessing. It's an act of gratitude.[2]

What makes his definition of work different from many others, says Fox, is the issue of joy. "There are two questions to ask about work. One, what joy does it give to you, the worker, and what joy does your work give others? Number two, in what way does your work relieve the pain and suffering of others?"

Role Models for Meaningful and Satisfying Work

All my life I have been blessed by knowing many people who personify Matthew Fox's definitions of meaningful and joyous work. From them I learned early that when spirituality is integrated with life, meaningful and joyous work naturally follow.

The first role models were my parents, both teachers in our small town of Shenandoah, Virginia (population about 3000). Evidence of their work was everywhere. The playground slide and merry-go-round had been built by my father's high school shop students; the high school plays were directed by my mother the English teacher. Both found ample time for community service and for creative pursuits. For my mom, this meant sewing draperies for churches, directing several church choirs, designing and sewing most of the family clothes, and writing music. For Dad, there was time for serving on the church board of deacons, attempting to write a great and saleable novel, and numerous creative woodworking projects.

From an early age, my brother Bill, sister Peggy and I were expected to work. While helping do dishes or working in the garden or building our own home, we gained an opportunity that children today often miss, which is learning firsthand the satisfaction of meaningful work.

We learned from our parents' stories that, no matter what others were doing, cheating just isn't an option. Their stories of ethical courage began with the time when Dad dared to turn down lucrative, unethical work at the height of the Depression. Soon after, he found work that led to a teaching position at the college where my mother was a student. When I was just a baby, Dad and a few colleagues blew a whistle against a powerful boss who was embezzling. Mom was Dad's major supporter during that hard time.

Woven into stories of challenge were stories of opportunity and hope, like the many people who had helped both of them work their way through college. And though Mom tended to be a workaholic, I can't remember a time when we were too busy working that we couldn't stop to appreciate the song of a mockingbird or the beauty of the mountains, particularly as the green and pink colors crept up the mountains each spring, then autumn colors crept down six months later. Nor did I ever think it was unusual if there was prayer in the midst of everyday life or an ethical discussion in the midst of hoeing a row of tomatoes.

While we definitely got the message that our parents' work was satisfying and valued, we didn't get any message that it was special. In that small town where everyone knew everyone else, we could see clearly the impact each person's work had on another. The doctor might get paid more than the milkman, but the milkman's work was just as necessary and he was greeted just as respectfully as the doctor. The owner of the hardware store and his clerks were equally appreciated for making available the things we needed when we needed them.

By the time I graduated from college in 1964, work had become more technically complicated. Soon, even in a small

town like Shenandoah, people would have difficulty understanding just what it was all their neighbors did for a living.

But I didn't spend much time in Shenandoah after high
school graduation in 1960, for everything had changed for
me in 1956 when my mother died. For a time I had thought
I was called to become a doctor and find the cure to her illness. After that dream collapsed in the first semester of pre-
medical studies, I felt guilty, not yet realizing that I had
never felt called to become a doctor. Instead, I had only been
swayed by unexpressed grief into the hope that by doing
something important, my life and my mother's death would
be meaningful. In the process of trying to avoid grief, I had
forgotten my parents' lessons that all honest work is meaningful, and that by working with meaning, there would
always be joy. There might not be party-hearty fun, but there
would be deep pleasure, sometimes expressed through
laughter, sometimes through the satisfaction of stretching
skills or creating relationships that were far more fulfilling
than anything that had previously been imagined.

Becoming actively involved with the spirit and work
movement since the mid 1990s has reconnected me with the
wisdom of my parents and added a whole new world of role
models. While gathering stories and photos about what I call
workplace altars (see chapter 3), I documented creative ways
people in many fields, at all levels of the corporate ladder,
are integrating their spiritual and work lives. This led to
writing articles about spirit and work for *Spirit at Work
Newsletter*, which led to writing twenty-six columns on spirit
and work for the *San Francisco Examiner & Chronicle*'s Career
Search Section.[3]

Thanks to these and other opportunities to write and
speak about everyday spirituality, I've been privileged to
interview many people who elegantly integrate their spiritual
life and their work-life. This includes people who are committed to specific faiths and those whose spirituality is eclectic or nonreligious. Some interviewees have little formal training in spirituality or religion; others, like world religions

scholar Huston Smith, author of *The Illustrated World's Religions: A Guide to Our Wisdom Traditions*,[4] make it their life's work. In a July 1998 interview, Dr. Smith said:

> Some people love their work and throw themselves into it. I am emphatically one of them. There is nothing I enjoy more than work, except relationships with family and taking the dogs for a walk and composting. Those are great pleasures. Other than that, there is no line between work and play because I like to create and my work gives me ample time for that.[5]

Huston Smith considers himself fortunate because he gets to do work he loves "within the context of supporting relationships." He's a perfect example of what many mean by meaningful work. His tasks derive from his talents and passions, and what he does is recognized as meaningful by others.

But meaningful work is not limited to job description or even a match among talents, passions, and tasks. The most important determinant is attitude, followed by ethical action.

Patsy Attwood works as a station agent in an underground rapid transit station not far from Huston Smith's home. She also considers herself fortunate because she does work she loves within the context of supporting relationships.

Attwood's job description includes helping lost travelers find their way or deal with jammed farecard machines. What she calls her "ministry" is to pray for all who pass by. The way she does this makes her love her work. It also helps her handle stress gracefully, provide excellent customer service, and end her day with abundant vitality and time for a fulfilling personal life.[6]

A Role Model for Your Own Meaningful and Joyous Work

From Patsy Attwood, Huston Smith, and other interviewees come a model for work-life excellence that anyone can follow. This model assumes that meaning and joy can be found whenever you choose to live and work more consciously and attuned to God's will. It begins when you awake and, instead of rushing to the shower or the morning paper, you take time to reflect and focus on what matters.

Maybe in the beginning, you find time only to say to yourself, "I welcome divine inspiration for my day," or some other short prayer. Then, through prayer, you gradually find more effective and satisfying ways to enliven and unite body, mind, and spirit while you do your morning chores.

All day, you treat obstacles as opportunities for learning and growing. You treat others respectfully, as if they were Jesus or Buddha or Allah or whoever has deepest meaning for you.

Throughout your day, you ask yourself questions such as:

- How can I work compassionately and ethically from my faith and values, not leave them in the parking lot and turn a blind eye to business practices I abhor?
- What can I do when I hate my job?
- How can I identify my talents and see what I am called to do with them, then obtain a job that best uses these talents?
- How can I fulfill vocational calls while still meeting current needs and obligations, including family and current employer?
- How can I know and follow God's will through my work?

Such moments of prayer and reflection help you anchor yourself in that which is most meaningful. They help you work more effectively and end your day refreshed, ready for a fulfilling homelife. Rest then prepares you for another cycle of satisfying work and life.

In this model, meaning and work are no longer divided. Instead, the two "hands," work and life, now roll into and support each other. Through your prayer and other spiritual practices, you anchor yourself into the source of meaning, and you gain guidance on how to work and live with meaning.

Through your conscious and compassionate work, you shape meaning into acts of creativity and compassion, which stretches and enhances your spiritual life.

In Michelangelo's painting in the Sistine Chapel of God and Adam, God extends a finger towards Adam, bestowing life. At the points where your fingers touch each other, imagine the source of all meaning—which ultimately is God—giving life to the creator in you.

Notice how these touchpoints are supported by the rest of you. Your opposable thumbs allow you to create and use tools that nonhuman creatures cannot. Your arms can draw what is needed, push away what is not.

Your heart beats not just your physical vitality but also messages from your soul. Your multiple intelligences include rational left brain, image-making right brain, and gut instincts. These connect to other intelligences throughout your nervous system, organs, and every cell of your body. Your legs anchor you in current reality and allow you to explore a world filled with possibilities.

God designed all these parts to help you do work that is nothing less than excellent, nothing less than meaningful, nothing less than satisfying. A big part of your life task is to discover all these parts and help them work together in the service of yourself and others.

In your quest for meaningful work, you will undoubtedly need support. Until recently, it was hard to find much wisdom for meaningful work, other than advice about vocational planning or ethics, for the prevailing attitude was that spirituality or religion was on the one hand, and work or business was on the other. How then could there be any meaningful discussions about work?

Understanding the Fear of and Longing for Spirit at Work

Yet, even when discussions about spirituality were considered taboo at work, people held secret discussions. In the summer of 1976, when I "temped" at a commercial real estate firm in Washington, D.C., every executive but one and every staff member but one got me alone, off site or behind closed doors, to talk about spirituality.

First they all demanded secrecy, believing that no one else in the firm would understand. I was different, they said, because I talked openly about my interest in spirituality. They also trusted me to keep their secrets.

Margaret, the receptionist,[7] admitted that she hid a Bible in her desk and prayed frequently. Gina, the mailroom manager, used prayer and poetry to help heal from near-suicidal depression. Mike the researcher had studied Buddhism and visited the spiritual community of Findhorn in northern Scotland.

My temporary boss told me what he'd rather do than sell commercial real estate. A vice president had questions about meditation. An executive wanted to discuss how difficult it is to live his values in a corporate setting.

During other temporary jobs that I took to supplement writing projects, I discovered that if I was covering for someone who would return, the desk drawers almost always hid revelations about the employee who was away: sacred scriptures, inspirational poetry and quotes, religious symbols or photos.

Recently, conversations about spirit and work have moved out of hiding throughout the business world, while spiritual items have moved out of hiding places in desk drawers and into places of honor on many desktops. Such conversations and objects have become numerous, and they evidence increasing openness to insights from other traditions and to personal creativity.

In *The Next American Spirituality*,[8] George Gallup, Jr., and Tim Jones note that today's worldwide spiritual revival is increasingly ecumenical and concerned with spirituality in everyday life. "In light of the rediscovery of 'everyday' spirituality," they say, "it is no surprise to find that Americans take this newfound sense to their workplaces. Many in our survey, when asked, said the first thing they thought about upon waking was work."

After asking, "Did you have occasion to talk about your religious faith in the workplace in the last forty-eight hours?" Gallup and Jones report that in one survey, "forty-eight percent said they had—almost half! For many, that may have been no more than a quiet, 'I will be praying for you' when told of a colleague's upcoming surgery or medical test. But the answer is striking. It suggests that Americans no longer see the workplace as cordoned off from spiritual concerns."[9]

In a telephone interview about the book, Gallup said that many people lack courage to come out of hiding in the spiritual woodwork with those concerns. Each person who does so, he said, helps embolden others. "If you give a testimony or prayer, people say 'ah!' as if they've been given permission."

Jones said that a major problem is perception. When he asks workshop participants whether they have experienced God's presence in their lives, the majority say they have. Yet few believe that others have had such an experience and could understand.

Today there is a dizzying array of options for discussing spirit and work. There are books, conferences, discussion groups, and websites that focus on different aspects of spirituality and work. Thanks to feature articles about spirit and work in business magazines such as *Forbes*, *Industry Week*, *Workforce*, *Training*, and the *Wall Street Journal*, it's practically impossible for business people not to notice that there's been a major shift in public perceptions of spirituality and its place at work.

Even so, fears of speaking about spirit and work persist. Among the concerns that are routinely voiced in discussion groups around the world are questions such as:

- Will spirit weaken my effectiveness, especially my ability to compete in a tight market?
- Will I look foolish or flaky to co-workers, clients, or competitors?

- How can I set appropriate boundaries, so one worker's expression of religious values respects another's longing to be left alone?

All these are valid questions that will be considered throughout this book. They should be carefully explored over time by anyone who chooses to integrate spiritual life and work life. Like most meaningful issues, they do not always lend themselves to quick, easy answers.

Fears and concerns about spirit and work are heightened by the fact that people tend to distort how they assess the beliefs and actions of others. With people from other cultures or religions—especially those we have been taught to fear or hate—it's easy to generalize and homogenize. Although we see ourselves as capable of change, it's easy to assume that They will always be this way or that. Though we recognize the diversity within our own groups, we assume that They are all alike. Without dialogue that allows the meeting of diverse hearts and minds, such distortions will persist. These fears intensify whenever we confuse spirit (which all of us have in common) with religions (which often divide us).

Just What Is Spirituality and What Is Its Place at Work?

As discussions about spirit and work become common, so do debates about the meaning of spirit. This leads to other debates about spirituality and religion and what constitutes authentic spirit and work.

This book will not end this debate, and it is definitely not meant to substitute for discussion or study within your own religious tradition. Hopefully, however, the following discussion will help you be true to your own faith.

One way to describe spirit is as the essence of the Creator and the created. Spirit includes the divine spark that makes us uniquely ourselves, yet most connected to God and all creation. Spirituality can be seen as whatever we do to meet, tend, develop, and express our spirits in the world and with God. Spirituality includes commonly accepted practices such as praying, creating rituals that help us know and honor the divine, and performing acts of mercy. It sometimes also includes "nonspiritual" practices such as psychology, which allows us to understand ourselves and liberate our true gifts.

Religion is the particular combination of beliefs and practices that shape our spirituality and join us with others in common worship. Religion is the particular discipline that helps us discern what matters most and helps us base our lives on principles of ultimate meaning.

For many, religion is defined by written scriptures; for others, it is not. For many, religious practices are defined by respected authorities; for others, the only valid authority is the alignment of one's inner core with the divine.

David Welbourn, a British industrial chaplain,[10] spent his fall 2000 sabbatical studying the theory and practice of spirituality in U.S. corporations, then applying his findings to a theological appraisal. His sabbatical report notes two types of definitions of spirituality. "There is the type designed to satisfy adherents of a particular faith. And there is the type that is suitable in business organisations where people of all faiths and none are to be found. In the latter context, a definition should serve, among other things, to bind people more closely together in their common task."

Welbourn believes that both types of definition are needed. "So whatever our personal faith background and spiritual emphases, for the purpose of promoting spirituality and work, we need to agree on a definition that is capable of embracing us all. Such a definition is almost bound not to reflect precisely our own spiritual tastes. Compromise is essential."

There probably always will be a natural tension between spirituality and religion. Without context, such as the scripture and rituals that shape many religions, spirituality can be vapid. Without community and its demands for discipline, spirituality can be lost in individualism or illusion.

At the same time, it takes constant work to keep spirit alive once religion enters the picture. Religions, however divinely inspired, are interpreted by people who have faults. Just as people have varied needs for psychological or creative growth, they also have varied needs for spiritual growth.

All spiritual practices and religions can be distorted. The Bible was once used by some to justify slavery; the Koran is now being twisted by some to justify terrifying vendettas. Spiritual practices and traditions can be trivialized. Religious authority, like political authority, can be misused.

Authentic Spirituality at Work

The spirituality-at-work movement can fall into all spiritual traps. In a 1995 paper for the Organizational Development Network, Mike Bell spoofs these distortions as, "We take three ccs of spirituality, or have a spirituality 'power lunch,' and we believe we'll compete more effectively and be happier doing it. When all else fails, try prayer."[11]

Bell's paper concluded with "Top Ten Reasons Why Managers Don't Like to Get into the Realm of Spirit." This list does a great job of nailing the fears and foibles of the spiritual journey at work. Some excerpts:

- *Sounds too much like church.* If someone starts talking about Spirit, people could start thinking about religion or God or something—and God knows where that will lead.
- *The language is too airy-fairy.* Too spooky. Not scientific enough. Can't shoehorn this kind of lingo into a policy statement or a management directive.
- *Too difficult to control. . . .* Too unpredictable to be of any practical value.
- *Sounds too much like "jock-talk."* With all the downsizing

and layoffs, and the flattening of structures and the casualties . . . too many "teams" have been wiped out. And this Spirit stuff is just a bit too close to telling people to "Get out and win one for the Gipper."

- *It is too much hard work.* You can't delegate it. You can't do it part-time. Too much personal accountability. You've got to live in Spirit and walk the talk, day in and day out.

Bell's spoof points to elements of authentic spirituality at work: allowing God to lead us beyond today's policy statements and management directives into places we cannot now imagine; trading cynicism for the hard work of real teamwork; being personally accountable; living and working in spirit, day in and day out.

The events of September 11, 2001, and afterward have shown us how profoundly many of us yearn to do just this. People who once never found a moment to pray or do community service suddenly found hours or days for both. Many left work to be with friends or families. Others found new meaning in work. Police officers and firefighters became our new heroes, and many of us asked, "What gives them courage to do what they do every day? What would it be like to have work worth dying for?"

In the seeds of these questions is another: "What would it be like to have work worth living for?"

When the chips are down, we all know what's truly meaningful and how to act with meaning. The challenge is to do that on a daily basis, so the work that takes up so much of our lives can be a rich source of meaning and joy. Fortunately, even hard work can be healing and enlivening.

Donna Reifsnider, a journalist who worked for the *Bowie Blade News* in Maryland, says that no one on the paper ever wants to have to cover an event so painful or to work so intensely as they did in the weeks after September 11. But they all want to maintain the new gifts that the crisis pulled out of them and their community. "I was glad to be a journalist at this time," she said. "I felt I had a window seat on the world, and everyone was deeply sharing the moment. Whoever I interviewed or photographed, they were not wary of me as a reporter because we all knew what we wanted and what we felt—and it was the same: we grieved for the lost, we wanted to be safe, we would be united."

Reifsnider's colleague Roxanne Powell worked through her fears and concerns about her own family, four of whom are in the service. Instead of going to Mass twice a week, she went daily for several weeks. Jennifer Martin, who's in her twenties, reported that the event made her more somber and aware of how short life is. She's determined to stop putting off things that matter to her. David Emanuel, the office wit, still has a great sense of humor, but he's become more pensive. Everything for him took on a new intensity and sense of vitality.

Reordering of priorities at work is common now, says George Gallup, for "events have pushed religion back into the public square. However, we don't know yet how this tremendous burgeoning in spirituality will become manifest. I'm concerned that though religious interest is broad, it is not very deep in terms of dealing with society's problems."

Gallup prays for a spiritual transformation that "brings people closer to God, to neighbor. If it helps people to get their priorities in order, away from materialism to something deeper, that would be wonderful; if it recognizes the evil that can lurk in the human heart, that is important."[12]

Dealing with issues like these at work requires us to learn to pray and cultivate a meaningful spiritual life in the midst of busy days. For most people, says Tim Jones, that is the only way it can happen. In *Awake My Soul: Practical Spirituality for Busy People*, Jones says he is constantly discovering the presence of God in the midst of chores like chauffeuring the kids or vacuuming. "Nothing, not even busyness," he writes, "need separate us from the love of God we long for. Not when God can be found in the midst of life itself."[13]

What about You?

How do you seek and find the presence of God in the midst of your most mundane work? How is your work now meaningful and joyous? How are you called to make it more so?

Each chapter in this book offers ideas and stories showing how people like yourself are answering these questions. Right now, I invite you to make one list of what's meaningful to you, and another list of whatever comes to your mind about work (positive and negative). Be specific. Rather than "horrible commute" or "great friend," say what makes the one horrible and the other great, such as "forty-five minutes each way on a crowded, noisy subway" or "her smile brightens my spirit all day." Review the list and edit it frequently.

For example, Juanita once listed "frequent spats with co-worker Bill" as a work challenge. After becoming more compassionate and assertive at work, she now lists "the joy of collaborating with Bill" on her list of what's meaningful.

Next, let one hand represent work and the other represent meaning. Maybe you'd like to draw symbols on the hand that represents meaning and joy, and symbols that represent work on the other. Move your hands until they symbolize the relationship between meaning and work for you right now. If they work well together, notice what helps them do that. If they're separate, notice what's driving them apart. Pray for guidance about what shifts in attitude or actions would unite meaning and work for you.

Experiment with this exercise throughout your workday and invite others to experiment with you. When you receive new guidance for meaningful work and life, record it and give thanks. Then pray for guidance to learn even more.

Accept the fact that answers to prayer do not always come quickly or lead to easy solutions. In his first book, originally published in 1972 but recently reissued and retitled *Prayer: A Radical Response to Life* (Tarcher, 2001), Matthew Fox defined prayer not as a request to God for answers or favors, but as an engagement with God in an ever-changing journey filled with questions. Sometimes we will be called to savor fully the wonder of Creation; other times, to experience emptiness and pain. By daring to be changed by the dynamic pulse of life and death and love, and by the mystery of what lies beyond, our compassion is stirred, our creativity enlivened.

Many of the joys and challenges of prayer come from the fact that prayer will always take us past our comfort zone. Many times we will be tempted, as Ebenezer Scrooge was in the beginning of Charles Dickens's *A Christmas Carol*, to mislabel the true voice of spirit as something like indigestion or foolish dreams. Other times, we will be tempted to deify our own faults or misperceptions.

Thus, discernment is always part of the spiritual path at work, as in the rest of life. Fortunately, all authentic spiritual traditions have developed excellent exercises for discerning what is true and what is not. A prime example is the collection of Spiritual Exercises of St. Ignatius, founder of the Jesuits, which are now being used by people of many faiths.[14]

Hopefully, this book will help you discern which practices are relevant to your spiritual work life and which are not.

As you begin your own exploration into the many possibilities for creating meaningful and joyous work, may you do so soberly. May you accept the fact that once you have seen the possibilities for meaningful and satisfying work, you will no longer settle for work that is soul-destroying or unethical. As you open all the eyes of your body, mind and spirit, may you see how even the hard times at work can lead to new growth and new possibilities for satisfying service, no matter what type of honest work you currently do.

1

Discovering New Possibilities for Meaning and Joy at Work

From my Grandmother Mary Stephenson Lee's kitchen comes a picture of what it means to work with meaning and joy. Although she often served "store-boughten" bread, at least once a day the hand-hewn bread trough was pulled out of a cupboard and placed on the countertop to the right of the sink. Into it were poured her ingredients. In the time-honored Southern way, no measuring utensils were used.

Mixing the ingredients was easy, but kneading the dough took hard and skilled effort. Starting at the front of the trough, Grandmother would press down with her palms while she rolled the dough away from her body, stretching its mass past several breaking points. Then gracefully, her fingers gathered the dough back toward her for many more cycles of fold and stretch, gather and reunite.

For Grandmother, the bread trough was a place of prayer. Here she worked out many of her troubles and worked in her blessings. Here she enfolded matter with meaning, then made it ready for transformation into a new form of love. It seems a perfect symbol for the process of enfolding any work with meaning and allowing both to be transformed.

Grandmother's spirit was also worked meaningfully into form in her garden, where she retreated after clashes during her seventy-two-year marriage to a man as strong-willed as herself. Whatever thoughts she worked out as she pulled weeds, she mostly kept to herself or to Grandaddy, but her gardens flourished for as long as she could tend them. So did the marriage, until her death at the age of ninety.

Southern women were once trained to keep their hands busy, even while visiting someone else's home. "Idle hands are the devil's workshop" was one popular saying. "A rolling stone gathers no moss" was another.[1] For Grandmother, busyness took shape through crochet. It was always fascinating to watch her take a plain ball of thread and turn it quickly into something else: doilies, large and small; a thick mat in popcorn stitch to keep Grandaddy's hair oil from staining the fabric of his rocker; tablecloths; bedspreads. Beauty.

She tried to teach me this craft. I learned enough to know that crochet is based on very simple maneuvers that can turn into complex patterns by subtly changing the way thread meets needle. I also learned that patience and an even rhythm made all the difference between my lumpy messes and Grandmother's elegant creations.

One of my most precious legacies from my grandmother is her dough trough. Another is her King James Bible, bought sometime in the 1920s and used at least into the mid 1970s. Held together with electrical tape, it bears the marks of decades of loving use. In its pages are various photos, clippings, and other items. Many people tell me that they also place items in their Scriptures as a way to pray over all they represent. I sometimes put the chapters of this book into Grandmother's Bible as a way to pray that these words from my mind and the meditations of my heart do her the honor she deserves.

My relationship with Grandmother was often difficult. I could be as stubborn as she was determined to direct me, particularly after my mother—her daughter—died when I was just thirteen. In many ways, our relationship was also a microcosm of the upheaval in the '60s and '70s. She stood for tradition, and she was not interested in talking about the things that most fascinated me, like diverse forms of spirituality, art, psychology, the civil rights and women's movements. To her and countless others like her, spirituality was meaningful only in the context of religion.

There were long periods when I thought Grandmother had nothing more to teach me, or that she could not possibly understand a spirituality that was meaningful to me if it was expressed differently from hers. Yet, the harder I tried to express the original intent of this chapter, the more memories of Grandmother interrupted my thoughts. By embracing these memories and praying over their meaning for many days, a new framework for talking about spirit and work evolved.

To be *authentic*, spirit at work has to be as accessible and ordinary as Grandmother's bread trough and crochet hook It has to be as strong and pliable as bread dough, so it can withstand many cycles of stretching and breaking. It has to be as simple to understand as basic crochet stitches, yet even more capable of being crafted into complex forms.

To be *useful*, spirit at work needs to be practiced until it becomes both a skill that can be engaged with minimal or no rational thought, and an opening of our consciousness to new wisdom that surpasses current understanding. Spirit at work has to be relevant to the task of the moment, while anchoring us in the eternal. It needs to be enfolded in the most authentic teachings that we know, then unfolded into our work.

The Drive for Meaning

However meaning is defined, the drive for meaning is so innate that it cannot be killed. Although it can be hidden from consciousness, there is always something in us that acts like plants that seek out the light and grow toward it.

In the busy and often cynical workplace, it's easy to forget how important meaning is in our lives. Psychiatrist Victor Frankl sheds light on this point. While imprisoned in Auschwitz during World War II, he discovered that no matter what others do to us, they cannot rob us of our attitudes and our ability to choose meaningful life and death. In *Man's Search for Meaning* and other books throughout an almost fifty-year post-war career, Frankl spread the message that meaningful experiences can spell the difference between satisfaction and despair, between stress and vitality, even between life and death.

Frankl called his work logotherapy (from the Greek *logos* or "meaning"). According to him, the human drive for meaning is basic. We find meaning, he says, "by creating a work or doing a deed; by experiencing something or encountering someone; and by the attitude we take toward unavoidable suffering. . . . We must never forget that we may also find meaning in life even when confronted with a hopeless situation."[2]

But what is meaning? How does one claim meaning? In a spring 1972 independent study project on the psychology of religion, conducted at Tufts University, Tracy Marks describes seven interpretations of meaning and how it is attained. For Frankl, she says, "meaning is experienced by responding to the demands of the situation at hand, discovering and committing to one's own unique task in life, and by allowing oneself to experience or trust in an ultimate meaning—which one may or may not call God."[3]

For many religious people, any definition of meaning would have to include a dedication to a particular faith, or at least a direct recognition of one's relationship to God. Thus, a Buddhist definition of meaning may be very different from one written by a practicing Hindu or Muslim. Then again, the definition may be both totally true to one's specific faith while being universal.

Rabbi Abraham Heschel is obviously Jewish. Yet, his writings have deep meaning for people of all faiths. Here is Tracy Marks's summary of Rabbi Heschel's definition of meaning, stated in a way that beautifully applies to meaningful work: "Man experiences his life as meaningful when he lives in God's presence—not simply by encountering God in the world, but primarily by serving God in everyday life, infusing every moment with the spirit of God, and by dedicating himself to ends outside himself."[4]

Finding Your Own Meaning

For spirit and work to be personally meaningful, it must reflect individual needs and express individual souls. Then it must be courageously claimed and practiced, even when external forces (including wise and loving grandmothers) appear not to approve.

There are many paths to discovering what's personally meaningful at work. Three universal and enduring ones include: 1) paying attention to our stories; 2) being conscious of and conscientious about our minute-to-minute choices; and 3) prayer. Here are some examples that show how others are exploring these paths at work.

Paying attention to our stories: The stories of our lives—our own personal stories and the stories of childhood and young adulthood—that have influenced us tell us a great deal about how we find meaning. Jane's and Lisa's experiences demonstrate discoveries of meaning in the details of their work lives.

Jane was raised by a father who trained her to be emotionally tough so she could survive in a competitive world and find meaning from money and career success. She learned to swallow disappointments and become a stellar performer.

In her first post-college job as catering manager for an elite hotel, she had to ensure that events ran smoothly. Sometimes she feared she might not be up to it all, especially when she doubted her ability to continue to treat herself like a spectacular results-producing machine.

In business school, Jane had been taught to see lower-level staff as predictable, self-interested, shortsighted, and not too smart. Managers had to be careful not to be overly concerned about staff needs lest they be distracted from producing bottom-line results.

Jane sought contradictions to this premise. Thus, she was able to appreciate the wisdom of the hotel's switchboard manager, a painter, and a carpenter, whom she joined for dinner one night in the employee cafeteria.

The peaceful tone of their conversation was drastically different from the hurried and pressured talk in upper-management meetings. Using words like "stewarding," not "managing," the three colleagues talked about treating staff and co-workers kindly. They also spoke about dealing calmly with difficult and unfair management mandates, with a slow and steady, one-day-at-a-time approach.

As she listened, Jane noted that for Genevieve, the switchboard manager, it seemed important to bear witness that she was Christian if the subject came up, but she was not out to promote her faith. Joe, the painter, demonstrated a sense of strong spirituality but an aversion to religion. Dave, the carpenter, revealed himself as steeped in various traditions that honor honesty and an appreciation of powers greater than ourselves. From him came an essence of humility without self-denigration.

After dinner, Jane told her colleagues, "It sounds to me like you guys are at church."

They laughed, then Genevieve smiled and said, "Jane, you can do your ministry anywhere."

That evening had a profound affect on Jane. "They gave me hope," she said recently. "Maybe there was a net to catch me if I failed. Maybe I didn't have to be so afraid, so intent and focused. Maybe I didn't have to move so fast. Maybe I could also be more humble and grateful. Maybe I could also exert my values into the world through my work."

Lisa's story leads us to another insight: it's not always easy to notice when workplace stories lead us away from meaningful work. As a top executive for a large corporation, Lisa once thought she enjoyed the "war stories" that she and her male colleagues told because they made her feel accepted in a world where women had long been excluded. She even engaged in the "who's-the-toughest" and "who-can-take-the-most-stress" bragging contests that were common in her company.

Then one day her boss bragged that he was so loyal to the company that he had missed the births of all four of his children. Everyone but Lisa laughed, for in that moment she woke up to the fact that success in this company just wasn't worth it. After much reflection about her values, she's now in divinity school.

Frankl taught that once we find the purpose in our lives and work, we can find the will and the way to fulfill our purposes with meaning. If this is true, then the most practical things in our work and lives aren't limited to logical tools like flow charts and measuring sticks. The most practical things also include practices that anchor us in meaning, then help us align our free will and our creative gifts with the source of ultimate meaning.

Sometimes meaningful practices are found in the midst of the mundane. Barbara Sher, author of *It's Only Too Late If You Don't Start Now: How to Create Your Second Life after 40* (Delacorte Press, 1998) and other great career books, said in a workshop many years ago that all the stories and movies we loved when we were growing up are important clues to what we find most meaningful. By imagining a conversation with early heroes, we can tap wisdom within ourselves that is often blocked. This phenomenon is akin to what happened when we played as children. Who wasn't at least a little more daring when playing Tarzan, a little confident when imitating Katherine Hepburn?

As children, we learned many stories that can inspire us today. *The Little Engine that Could*[5] reminds us that we can achieve unusual results when 1) we're motivated by compassion; 2) we have a positive vision; and 3) we stay on track. The little boy in Hans Christian Andersen's classic fairy tale of "The Emperor's New Clothes" reminds us that even the lowliest member of an organization has insights that are much needed by higher-ups who are too driven by fear or pride to see or tell the truth. That story also portrays how much an entire organization can suffer from fraud, waste, or abuse when it is organized around a leader's faults, not around a purposeful vision.

Nancy Drew, heroine of mystery books that have been popular for many decades, is a wonderful imaginary companion in the quest for meaningful work and life. She models these attributes:

- being attentive, so tiny clues can be seen clearly; reflecting about the meaning of clues without obsessing over them;
- being courageous in the search for truth, even when others place obstacles in the way;
- being compassionate and allowing others to share both the work and the rewards of the quest.

While recalling memorable childhood moments like a love of Nancy Drew, buried personal treasures can come alive again. It's as if, while transplanting insights from the back of our memory storehouse into the field of the present, we bring along some of the ground in which memories are planted: imagination, intuition, curiosity, and other gifts that tend to be quashed in the process of becoming adults. Becoming more like a little child again, we are better able to enter the everyday heaven of meaningful work (see Matthew 18:1–4).

Moment-to-moment choices: There is no sweeter heaven on earth than meaningful work, for some joys can be found only through work. Meaning can be found not just in the fruits of work (e.g., paychecks and benefits) or by working in vocations that best stretch our talents or meet our individual callings. Meaning is also a moment-to-moment choice that can be exercised by any person, any time, anywhere, simply by opening our hearts and minds, then exercising our inbred will for meaningful work and life.

Prayer: The most important formula for meaningful work I know is to pray for guidance and pay attention. As I discovered while doing a temporary secretarial job in 1976, the answers don't always make sense at first.

My boss then was a union executive who used poor grammar. He didn't care that I had an undergraduate degree in English from a top-rated college. All he wanted was the quick-and-perfect use of my fingers to type many letters on an old, noncorrecting Selectric typewriter. Although he expected no typographical errors, he would not let me correct his own errors in grammar or spelling. I felt angry and unappreciated. I wanted to quit immediately and search for more meaningful work, but I had to complete the assignment in order to pay pressing bills.

Using many tricks I had learned about stress release and relaxation, I tried to focus on the task at hand. And although that helped, it was not enough. Finally, I prayed.

My first attempt was on the order of "God, help me get away from this lousy boss." This was obviously so un-prayerful that, if God answered at all, it was through a quick remembrance of 1 Corinthians 13:1: "If I speak in the tongues of mortals and of angels but do not have love, I am a noisy gong or a clanging cymbal." Then came a reminder that if I wanted to find work that better used my talents, it was up to me to go out and find that work. Meanwhile, "Thy will be done applies here, too, Pat."

How could divine will possibly apply to typing grammatically incorrect letters?

The answer is actually very complicated, gained only after a lot of thought. Here are a few highlights:

- Humility is always good spiritual practice.
- Self-interest and preconceptions block the full truth of any situation. Compassion opens the eyes to new perspectives.
- Commitment to any ethical task, however mundane or imperfect, can be joyful.

When compassion and humility opened my eyes, I saw
the boss less through a glass darkly and more face to face
(see 1 Corinthians:13, King James version) and I discovered
that he saw his poor grammar as a unique style. Although no
grammarian would agree with that "style," he was actually
doing a very good job of fulfilling the work for which he had
been hired, even communicating with others.

When I told the story of working for the boss with poor
grammar, someone told me about a seventeenth-century
Discalced Carmelite monk named Brother Lawrence of the
Resurrection who practiced the presence of God through
such mundane tasks as washing dishes and sweeping the
floor. People often came to the monastery just to help him do
these tasks so they could also learn how to work with meaning and joy. Here's how Brother Lawrence described his
work:

> I turn over my little omelet in the frying pan for the love of
> God. When it is done, if I have nothing to do, I bow down to
> the ground and adore God from whom has come the grace
> to make it. Then I straighten up, more contented than a king.
> When there is nothing more I can do, it is enough to pick up
> a straw from the floor for the love of God.
>
> People look for methods for learning to love God. They
> desire to arrive by I don't know how many different prac-
> tices. They take great pains to remain in the presence of
> God by a quantity of means. Is it not much shorter and
> more direct to do everything for the love of God, to use all
> the tasks of one's situation, to give testimony of it, and to
> maintain His presence within us by this communication of
> the heart with Him? He has no fancy ways for this. One has
> only to go plainly and simply to him.[6]

Does this mean that the essence of spirituality and work
is that we should just learn how to accept awful jobs from
employers who don't appreciate us?

No, although sometimes spirit calls us to humble ourselves, just as it sometimes calls us to things much greater than we could have imagined on our own.

Expressing Your Own Spirit at Work

What about you? What have you learned about meaningful work from your own equivalent of the boss with poor grammar or Grandmother and her dough trough? What more could you learn if you saw through the eyes of forgiveness, self-respect, and compassion? If you practiced the presence of God in everyday tasks?

What new paths to joy and meaning might you discover if Nancy Drew or another ally (living, dead, real, or imaginary) helped you see work with fresh eyes and a creative, nonjudgmental heart?

As you work with these and other questions, you will undoubtedly discover many possibilities for working with spirit: perhaps a prayer partnership at work; perhaps a discussion or study group in your faith community; perhaps a multi-faith group in your field; perhaps something totally different. Whatever possibilities come to you, take them to prayer. Let your prayer come out of your heart or adapt this one:

> Oh, God, help me see how I am called to bless myself and others at work. Help me see my purpose in work and life. Help me heal and grow while I work, and help me to support the health and growth of others through my work. Amen.

You may wish to write your prayer in the form of an affirmation, such as this one.

> Every day, I discover new ways to work with increased integrity and purpose. I find abundant wisdom to guide my work in my own tradition, from other traditions, and

through the moment-to-moment guidance of my own soul. As I work, I enjoy stretching my talents. Through work, I deepen relationships with other people and the earth. Through my work, I bring joy to myself and others.

2

Seeing Your Work
as a Spiritual Journey

The stories we tell ourselves about work can significantly detract from or enhance the quality of meaning and joy at work. For example, if our story about work refers to an exhausting treadmill we dare not leave, how can we see options for another reality? Or if work is a march up the ladder of success, how can we relax and enjoy camaraderie when others are either competing with us or too far beneath us to be appreciated as equals? If work is God's ongoing punishment for all humans, how can our work be grounded in God's love? How can money and other fruits of our work be blessed?

A more fulfilling story, on the other hand, dwells in the notion that work is an integral part of a lifelong spiritual journey in which we give and receive blessing by meeting challenges with the help of fellow travelers who are as lost and broken as we are. In the process, like Dorothy and her companions in Oz, we develop treasures we may have thought we lacked: courage, love, intelligence, and the pathway home.

A spiritual journey is more than a trip. During my first summer job as a waitress at Virginia's Luray Caverns, I was struck by the vast differences in what tourists brought to their experience and what they took away.

By any measure, the sixty-four underground acres that make up the Luray Caverns are spectacular. Embedded in land that was formed over the course of several hundred million years, the caverns' colorful formations were created drop by drop as water seeped through limestone for more than a million years. All around can be seen water droplets that will eventually become part of new stalactites or stalagmites that grow at the rate of about one new inch every one to two hundred years.

One highlight on the tour is a rare moment of total darkness. Another highlight is a concert on an organ created by Pentagon mathematician and electronic scientist Leland W. Sprinkle, which taps out pure musical notes from stalactites over a three-and-one-half-acre area.

It takes effort not to be awed by such beautiful natural history, but some people managed to do so. One family came in so exhausted from "doing" Washington, D.C., the day before, plus the Skyline Drive and the Caverns that day, that no one in the family enjoyed their meal. The children were too busy fighting, the mother too busy trying to ignore the children or make peace, and the father too busy mapping out how they could drive a total of 175 miles and "do" Richmond and Williamsburg in the next two days. It was easy to imagine what would happen next with this family. Loaded with souvenirs that quickly would turn to clutter, they would continue to be consumed by their lives.

By contrast, another family wasn't trying to see too much in too little time. For them, "one inch of growth every one to two hundred years" was an invitation to ponder the measurement of their days beside something that had preceded them by hundreds of thousands of years, and would undoubtedly still be growing hundreds of thousands of years or more into the future. It was an invitation for the family to ponder questions like, "Why did God make something so beautiful, then hide it underground where people might never find it?" It was easy to imagine this family returning home refreshed and loaded with treasures, spiritual and material: shared memories, enhanced perspective, photographs, and perhaps gifts for friends and family that would help them enter into the joy and meaning of the journey as well.

Work as a Journey of Joy and Service

It is always a blessing to encounter people who meet their work journey as zestfully and joyously as that family met their journey into and out of the Luray Caverns. One of these is creative counselor Carole Peccorini of Sonoma, California. She describes the spiritual journey as an ongoing willingness to "venture into the unknown, enter openheartedly into deep relationship with all that is found there, and discover anew who I really am and how I relate with something bigger than myself."

Peccorini chose to be a spiritual journeyer as a child. "We moved a lot. Dad was in the Air Force, and he loved adventure. Also, when we were moving, my mother [who was physically and mentally ill] was too busy to terrorize me."

Peccorini's gifts of staying attuned to meaning in spite of hardship were fortunately well honed by the age of twenty-five. Then, within a two-week period, her husband left, her father died, and her mother was hospitalized in a comatose vegetative state. Peccorini was left with responsibility for her own toddler and two teenage siblings.

> I knew I had to do something more personally and financially fulfilling than keep working as a legal receptionist. If I had had the financial resources, I'd probably have become an art therapist, which would have taken at least six years of advanced study. Because I couldn't imagine how to do that and fulfill my responsibilities, I chose nursing, which would take less training and let me work anywhere. But I vowed to incorporate my interest in art and therapy into nursing, and that's what I did.

While working with battered children, Peccorini confronted her own history of being battered. As she healed, she was drawn to work in pediatrics. Working with dying children and their families gave her the courage to direct the first local hospice program. There, through moments of deep presence with patients, "I faced death and learned to help children sustain development in the face of loss."

Peccorini says she has always been drawn to

> . . . the way spirituality lives in the sensory world. When people are abstract and theoretical, they are empty and can't meet another human being. I remember being sent to a local hospital with several hospice staff after a bus crash severely injured many foreign tourists. Several ministers were also dispatched, according to our disaster plan, so we could care for the emotional and spiritual needs of family members.
>
> Since family members had not yet arrived, we nurses began tending passengers who were less injured or even uninjured. As we worked, we talked.
>
> When television cameras arrived, they recorded the ministers sitting alone, waiting for people to come to them. In the center of the room, nurses sat knee to knee, counseling passengers one by one. Because we met them personally, we were the ones they turned to for living, breathing spiritual help that night.

Peccorini noticed that several ministers looked frozen, as if they didn't know what to do, and she felt concerned that she didn't know how to help them be useful. How could she help direct them in the event of a bigger disaster, such as an earthquake, when she was expected to count on their help?

Peccorini had previously offered hospice training to different community groups. That year she opened new training to clergy. Several attended and loved it. "They just needed to be supported in learning how to respond in a personal, direct way. To this day, program participants tell me it was a meaningful experience and they still use our training manual."

Peccorini says she still practices skills and attitudes she developed in her first teenage job, selling root beer at a drive-in. "That job taught me how to step out into a world of serving people one by one," she says. "I'll never forget that people have a basic thirst. I remember that Bible verse, 'I was thirsty and you gave me something to drink,' whether the basic thirst is for water or attention to some other basic need."

Like Peccorini, Presbyterian minister Eileen Epperson of Georgetown, Kentucky, learned some of her best spiritual practices long ago while doing what is normally considered mundane work. Before being clear about her call to ministry, Epperson was an assistant in an executive search firm. "Before that job," she says, "I thought business people didn't have a soul. I thought slogans like 'We care for you' on a company truck were just baloney. Then I saw how my boss worked with pleasure and accomplishment. She clearly cared about me and wanted the best from me. Because she believed in me, I found I had abilities I didn't know I had."

Epperson's boss taught her to serve people well by taking care of small details. "I couldn't just send a package. I had to call afterward, see if it had arrived, and ensure that it met the client's needs." As a minister, Epperson often applies basic listening and customer service habits like these. "That boss in the search firm showed me how people can work for God in any field. They can serve the good, and their work can be an expression of love and devotion."[1]

Epperson finds that seeing work as a spiritual journey empowers people by turning problems into grist for the mill. "Rather than feel victimized or overwhelmed by circumstances like a problem with workmates or some integrity issue, I can go within. Maybe I'll have to face some arrogance or selfishness. But if I see a challenge as my personal journey of growth to God inside the context of work, I can see more about myself and the actions I need to take."

Returning Blessing for Blessing

In a spiritual journey, work strategies are based on a deeper motivation than "How can I get what I want?" Instead, while meeting our own needs, we serve by giving what is inside of us to the rest of the community. Thus, in Matthew Fox's earlier words, we "return blessing for blessing."

Every culture has a concept of blessing that basically says, "I see you, not who I fear you are or who I wish you to be. I wish you well and envision the best for you. I will engage with you in a relationship where either or both of us can be changed."

Blessing is essential to seeing problems and challenges as grist for the mill. Problems that are cursed inevitably grow more difficult; problems that are blessed can be seen more easily in their fullness. As an unknown author puts it:

> Bless those who challenge us to grow, to stretch, to move beyond the knowable, to come back home to our elemental and essential nature. Bless those who challenge us for they remind us of doors we have closed and doors we have yet to open.

As I was reflecting recently on the concept of work as blessing, the following visualization emerged:

> Imagine that before your birth, the Creator laid his hands on the top of your head and said:
>
> *Behold, I give you a seed from my heart. It is my will that every time you feel your heart beat, you remember your connection to me and to all of creation.*
>
> *In your heart is a seed from my eye, that you may have vision. It is my will that you use your vision to see clearly who you are and what you are called to do in your life.*
>
> *In your heart are the seeds of a language that only you are to know, for it is to become the language of your own heart. Only you can shape this language through your perspective, your experiences, your dreams, and your deeds.*
>
> *In the heart of your hands are the seeds of work. Your first work is to exercise your heart, to develop your many visionary potentials, and to become fluent in the language of your own heart.*

Your life's work is to use all these gifts in the service of your-self and others. It will not be easy to do this, for I send you into a world where you will be surrounded by many who have forgotten the blessings I have given them.

Imagine that your task now is to rediscover and develop the blessings that are your birthright. Imagine that your work is part of a lifelong spiritual journey, in which every moment can be enlightening.

Spiritual Journey: Many Journeys in One

A spiritual journey includes many journeys, several of which may occur simultaneously. If this seems overwhelming, remember how you already play many different roles in life: father or mother, daughter or son, sister or brother, colleague, group member, casual acquaintance, student, mentor. Each of these roles shapes your life over time by offering different perspectives, opportunities, and challenges. Each role shapes the others. Similarly, the various spiritual journeys of work touch and transform one another.

While taking on the journey of facing your faults and creating work built on integrity, you will undoubtedly undergo the journey of building community through your work and revisioning your work or profession. In addition to these journeys, which are the subject of later chapters, there are many other ways to frame your spiritual journey at work. Here are a few:

The journey of vocation: The best known spiritual journey for work is the journey of vocation, from the Latin *vocare* or "call." In a totally secular sense, the vocational journey involves discovering and practicing the work that best fulfills our dreams and utilizes our unique talents. In a deeper spiritual sense, the vocational journey involves hearing and fulfilling a divine call about the particular service that best fulfills our purpose on earth and God's will for our lives.

The process of discovering vocation is often difficult, for it involves the in-depth interplay of self-awareness, personal passion, and listening to the voice of God in our lives. As such, it is already the subject of much prayer and of many therapy or vocational counseling sessions, great books, discussions with friends, and workshops.

Several problems arise when we limit our thinking about vocation to finding and performing a specific type of work. Do we pressure ourselves always to use every one of our best potentials or move up the ladder as high as possible, so that we fail to appreciate the worth of humble work or the need for occasional fallow times in our work lives? Do we assume that, once we've found the right job, our vocational journeying is done and we never again have to reflect or pray about what we are called to do?

Like the journey of human love, the process of discovery and initial commitment—however exciting and profound—does not negate the need for continuing recommitment to be as present to mundane and tough times as to creative and exciting ones. Thus, in the arena of meaningful work, as in the world of love, a pauper with limited education may actually find more satisfaction than one whose education or worldly wealth is used as a block to spiritual wealth and wisdom.

The journey of following a fascination: From the time he became a legal journalist in the late '80s, Steven Keeva heard the pain of lawyers. Numerous articles about the lack of civility and collegiality identified surface problems, but Keeva sought deeper roots.

Then, in 1996, Keeva found in his mailbox a brochure advertising a spirituality-and-work conference. Excited by this new notion of spirit and work, he surveyed the many books about the subject and began exploring how this might relate to the field of law. He soon met Rob Lehman, president of the Fetzer Institute in Kalamazoo, Michigan, which has sponsored programs to help lawyers reclaim their traditional roles as wise counselors, including contemplative law retreats that bring a variety of meditation practices to attorneys and law students. Lehman told Keeva that law is the tissue that holds together the outer life of the community. Out of that discussion came a realization that much of the pain in the legal field was due to the fact that the profession did not recognize the relevance of the inner life to lawyers. "If the inner life of lawyers is neglected, then lawyers lack access to their inner lives when dealing with clients," says Keeva. "This eventually has to be unsatisfying to everyone, including families, for it's hard for lawyers to leave their professional personas behind when they go home."

Keeva began interviewing lawyers and soon became convinced that lawyers, like members of other professions,

> . . . need to dip into the place of being face to face with God, to stand naked, being who you are and have some respite from all the assumptions and mindsets that imprison you. From this place, you can give your clients the profound gift of truly seeing them. Out of a very human collaboration with them can come truly satisfying work.[2]

In August 1999 Keeva's book *Transforming Practices: Finding Joy and Satisfaction in the Legal Life*, sponsored by the *Journal of the American Bar Association*, was launched at the national convention of the American Bar Association. The book, along with his website, www.transformingpractices.com, have become a beacon not only for those who want to reclaim the spirit of the legal profession but also for members of other professions.

The journey of personal growth and development: To be human is to grow. Long after our bodies add new height and adult teeth, our psyches stretch. It is in our nature to want to learn and to develop our many capacities: teacher as well as learner, leader as well as follower, fighter as well as peacekeeper, creator as well as appreciator of others' creativity.

All of the psychological issues that make human growth and development so challenging and interesting apply to

work. The gifts we developed as children at home or on
the playground — getting along well with others, enjoying
our own viewpoint, discipline, courage, risk taking, etc. —
will be further stretched and developed on the job. The
inhibiting habits we developed as children at home or on the
playground — being bossy or being intimidated by others'
bossiness, crumbling to peer pressure, blaming, etc. — will be
further challenged at work.

Bonnie Bell, M.Div., a career counselor in Oakland,
California, sees career development as a braiding of psychological, spiritual, and professional issues.

> People want to change because they are in pain about
> work, like they hate their job or are dissatisfied with their
> industry or they don't have enough authority. To find a
> career in which their personal, professional, and spiritual
> selves resonate, they must deal with the "voices" of their
> psyches. Otherwise, they're driven by them.

However, our psychologically oriented culture often
encourages people to get lost in their psychology. Thus,
many people don't allow self-knowledge to help them shape
a vision for life and work.

The basic visioning question, "What do you want?" may
seem trivial, but it is actually profound and difficult says
Bell. Many people can't answer this question or find joy in
work because they allow problems like low self-esteem to
cloud the lens through which they view life. By contrast,
strong self-esteem is based not on selfish pride but on
authenticity and self-respect. This makes room for dialogue,
for creativity, for growth both professionally and spiritually.
In this way, we live out Jesus' commandment to love others
as we love ourselves.

Bell recalls a competent social worker, Wanda, who
wanted out of the field because she felt unable to affect situations she found unjust. Then Wanda uncovered a belief that

her own needs weren't as important as the needs of others, and that she didn't deserve to have work she loved. Under that was a longing for more authority. "I want to be teaching, supervising, setting just policies," she said. Today Wanda directs a social service agency where she sets and administers just policies. Her good and joyous work ripples outward to clients and the people her clients affect, to friends and family, to the larger society, and to God.

The journey of co-creating a meaningful world: Whatever our work, we are called to co-create with God a world that is just and loving. According to Elizabeth O'Connor:

> In every person is the creation story. Since the first day of our beginning, the Spirit has brooded over the formless, dark void of our lives, calling us into our existence through our gifts until they are developed. And that same Spirit gives us the responsibility of investing them with him in the continuing creating of the world. . . . When we deny our gifts, we blaspheme against the Holy Spirit whose action is to call forth gifts. . . . A primary purpose of church is to help us discover our gifts and, in the face of our fears, to hold us accountable for them so we can enter into the joy of creating.[3]

An everyday reminder of the joy of creating is the Post-it Note, which was developed when choir singer Arthur Fry chose to pay attention to possibilities and play with them over time. The soundbite version begins with the moment a piece of paper Fry used to mark his place fell out of his hymnal, and he was unable to find his place before the song ended. This inspired him to create a moveable bookmark by applying a "failed" glue (one designed by 3M colleague Spence Silver that didn't stick well) to a piece of paper.

The rest was not, as some assume, immediate history. Like most stories, it had roots and context, some of which began in 3-M's long history of fostering innovation by allow-ing scientists time to work on pet projects without immedi-ate regard for the bottom line; by respecting "mistakes" or "failures" as part of the creative process; and by encouraging dialogue among staff. Thus, when Spence Silver invented a glue that "didn't stick well" (a low-tack glue) in a company known for quality adhesives, he had no reason to withhold his findings.

At any moment Fry could have dropped the inventive ball. When he first thought about the failed glue after losing his place in the hymnal, his first impulse was to forget it. But he chose to become fascinated with the possibility of creat-ing a moveable bookmark so he could always find his place when it came time to stand with the rest of the choir.

Next Fry tested his ideas. Because Silver's glue left a residue on the hymnal pages when Fry removed the first yel-low stickies, he created an even lower-tack glue. Next, he built a machine to put the glue on pieces of paper in the fam-ily basement. (Obviously, family support was critical to this creative process.) Only then did he consider the financial bottom line by asking secretaries, receptionists, and man-agers to help find better applications than a removable book-mark. Selling the product to the marketing department took persistence and faith; convincing the company to create new marketing strategies when the first tests were a flop took even more faith and persistence.[4]

Why aren't all of us as persistent as Arthur Fry in bring-ing our full creativity to the creation of meaningful and joyous work? Why don't we regularly enter into the creative process and, like the dough in Grandmother's trough, allow our essence to be worked and transformed into new forms of love?

The fact is that creating is so scary that we are tempted to yield to the culture's siren calls to give up and forget about our creative potentials. And, in fact, we do give up some of them long before we are able to utilize those potentials to create meaningful work.

Elizabeth O'Connor reports a study showing that 90 percent of the population measures "high creativity" at the age of five. "By the age of seven the figure has dropped to 10 percent. And the percentage of adults with high creativity is only two percent."[5] Surely the Creator did not intend our abilities to be so disposable!

But a child's sense of self is fragile, and it doesn't take much to cripple that sense of self and all the gifts it contains. Here are some painful moments some of my clients recall:

I loved drawing until my mother judged my work harshly. I stopped drawing.

I wrote a poem. The class bully found it and read it aloud. Everybody laughed. I stopped writing.

I told my father things that mattered to me. He got mad. Now I realize that some of my questions made him confront things he didn't want to see. Then I just felt hurt and scared. I stopped questioning.

I overheard my mother telling my secret to someone else, prefaced by, "Let me tell you about the latest dumb thing Tom did." I stopped trusting.

Creativity is just one of many gifts quashed in childhood. Others include wonder, intuition, and bodily instincts such as danger signals, and curiosity. But like the drive for meaning, these gifts can never be destroyed. Rather, they are merely hidden in unconscious sections of body, mind, and spirit. Some gifts will return to consciousness as work challenges pull out of us gifts we had forgotten. Other gifts may need to be uncovered carefully and deliberately, as if we were archaeologists seeking lost treasures.

For earthly archaeologists, primary tools include shovels, picks, and brushes. For archaeologists of the human spirit, tools include prayer, storytelling, psychotherapy and personal growth work, dreamwork, and various forms of the arts.[6]

It's not necessary to be an artist to use the arts as a pathway to liberating creative gifts. For example, people who want to reclaim their lost spontaneity may find much of it in an experiential theater group or a poetry writing class. Others may find pounding and shaping clay (without any concern for how "good" it is) is the doorway to a lost sense of wonder and the joy of creating.

The journey of receiving and leaving legacies: How shall we allow our elders to shape our work? What shall we learn from them and what shall we choose to unlearn? What legacies and gifts shall we leave through our own work?

Answers to these questions are often tangled in parent-child relationships, in which neither party is perfect. Susan once saw her mother as having nothing left for herself after sacrificing all she had for her children and students. When the work of raising and teaching children was done, Susan's mother become depressed, as if she no longer had a purpose. Susan says:

> When I vowed not to be like her, I shut down my naturally giving nature and that didn't serve me or anybody else. After many years of writing angry poetry, then channeling that anger into deeper creativity, I discovered that to live a full, passionate life I have to be more generous, like my mother. But I don't have to model how she gave herself in the world. By taking care of myself, I can better serve my son. When one purpose is fulfilled, I can seek a new purpose.

Susan recently built an altar for her mother for a local Dia de Los Muertos (Day of the Dead) ceremony. In the family basement, in a box she hadn't known existed, Susan found some of her mother's classroom lesson plans and artwork. While creating and exhibiting the altar, Susan felt as if her mother's spirit was helping her embody generosity while strengthening her own gifts.

No matter how wonderful our parents are or were, we are called to walk our own paths as we honor those who came before us — and that takes courage. Rhena Schweitzer Miller, the only child of Albert Schweitzer, was born into the challenge of having a father who was world-famous. For decades before and years after he received the Nobel Prize for Peace, he topped world polls for "most admired person." (For more about Schweitzer and his impact on the world, see chapter 9.)

But Miller found it difficult growing up in her father's shadow, for "everyone had such great expectations." On her fourth birthday, she thought the large number of visitors were there to see her. But most were really celebrating her father's birthday (the same day as hers), and "I realized that my father was not like the fathers of most of my friends."

Miller says she never suffered the pain of children of the famous (even children of those who are renowned only in small communities) because she learned early that "if I am my own person, then I live quite happily within myself without thinking I have to emulate."[7] Miller acknowledges that such an attitude is "un-American," but it is because of such attitudes that she can carry some of her father's legacy as lightly as if it were a chiffon scarf.

For those of us who have felt burdened by idealized images of all we must accomplish or who have difficulty finding a balance between self-care and the call to service, Miller's example of self-acceptance and good humor can be a great blessing. Indeed, the more lightly we can carry our ancestors' legacies, the more gracefully can we discover our own gifts and enrich the legacies we leave for others.

The journey of entering the darkness: Spiritual journeys are not easy rides. Many joys come only when we dare travel through what St. John of the Cross (1542–1591) calls the "dark nights of the soul," in which there is "no other light and guide than that which burned within my heart."[8]

St. John was a priest and member of the Carmelite religious order, one of many Roman Catholic communities of men or women who are dedicated to the service of God. One expression of this dedication is committing to a lifetime of poverty, chastity, and obedience.

During John's lifetime, Christian Europe was in turmoil. In addition to the Protestant Reformation, which had begun in 1517, there were numerous reform movements within the Catholic Church and its orders. At the urging of Teresa of Avila, a Carmelite nun, John became a vocal proponent of a call for the order to become more ascetic and contemplative, and therefore closer to its original ideals. He and Teresa, like many others, thought religious life had become too lax, without enough time for prayer and penance.

Due to a variety of religious politics and misunderstandings, John was thrown for several months into his monastery's jail. Then he was moved into a tiny, dark, lice-ridden, nearly airless room for almost ten months with only his Breviary (a collection of prayers that were to be said every day) for company. Like other religious leaders in our time, notably Martin Luther King, Jr., Nelson Mandela, and Mohandas Gandhi, John found the deprivation to be spiritually and creatively liberating.

This ability to use hardships as a catalyst for breakthrough to new wisdom is what many of us commonly think of as "the dark night of the soul," but John had another definition. He speaks of moments when even practices like prayer, which once brought consolations such as hope or feelings of oneness with God, don't seem to "work." It's as if, whatever direction is gained at the peak of a mystical experience or in the depths of guidance, there currently are no signs of being on the right track.

Dark nights call us to surrender to faith in the darkness itself. In the darkness, we are no longer dazzled by the lights of paths we once were called to trod. Rather, in the dark, the faint light of the new path can be more clearly seen. In the dark, new spiritual roots can grow.

Darkness is a common symbol for pain. In ancient tribal traditions throughout the world, as well as in modern psychotherapy circles, the most gifted healers are typically "wounded healers" who have gone deeply inside a particular pain and know it intimately. Only those with the wisdom gleaned from such personal experience can call forth the healing that is needed.

One very delightful wound healer is David Roche. Born with a horrible facial disfigurement that was made worse by medical intervention, Roche used humor to heal himself. Now, as the self-proclaimed minister of the Church of 80% Sincerity, he gives performances that help people face their own disfigurements and imperfections. His messages are particularly touching to adolescents, who tend to be obsessed with outer appearance.

As Rev. Dave says in "My Face Does Not Belong to Me"[9] :

The face is the locus of the human persona. At the deepest level, a distorted face can signify that God or the universe may be quirky and careless, or at worst, vengeful and punitive. When others judge a face to be marred, it serves as an unconscious reminder to them that the whole human experience, including their own, is one of being flawed.

I believe that seeing and accepting one's "flawed" condition is a core spiritual growth experience, the essential step in developing emotional maturity for all people, disabled and otherwise. . . . To survive spiritually and emotionally, I have been forced to find my own inner beauty. I have discovered that I am a child of God. I am whole. And my face is a gift, because my shadow side is on the outside, where I have had to deal with it. Paradoxically, I have been made whole through, and with, what originally seemed to be my flaws.

The journey of earning and spending money: One of the most common yet least recognized spiritual journeys is discovering and fulfilling the meaning of money. Money is a major reason we take jobs, even when we don't want to. Money affects how we spend our time, how we treat others (including the earth), and how others treat us. It affects whether or not we will have the courage to stand up to fraud and abuse at work, and whether or not we will follow the calls of spirit in our lives.

If money were just money, says psychotherapist and author of *Money Harmony* Olivia Mellan, "People could make rational choices about it. Instead money is a coverup for other issues, including love, power, security, fear, control, happiness, freedom, and independence."[10] All these issues played out in our families, and they still play out in the mixed messages about money in our culture.

One popular interpretation of Jesus'saying that it is harder for a rich man to get into heaven than for a camel to pass through the eye of a needle (see Matthew 19:24) is that it is inherently wrong to have wealth. Others say the verse is a lesson about humility based on the tradition that to go through the ancient gate called the Eye of the Needle, camels had to be stripped of their packs and crawl on their knees. Another interpretation is that the verse reminds us that spiritual life demands we sacrifice whatever gets in the way of meaning.

To uncover beliefs and distortions about money, Mellan suggests placing money on the table and having a dialogue with it. Record what you say and what you imagine money says to you. Imagine parents, spouses, important people at work, and God having dialogues with money. As you become more conscious about how your attitudes and beliefs about money interact with others' attitudes and beliefs, you are better prepared to make more meaningful choices.

The journey of the moment: This is ultimately the most powerful journey, for now is the only moment we inhabit. As

Brother Lawrence of the Resurrection demonstrated in the seventeenth century, we don't have to go anywhere or do anything unusual to practice the presence of God through work. Simply by being fully present to each task and working with love, we walk into sacred depths through the doorway of the mundane. In each moment, each breath, we are called to walk through that doorway anew. Thus, even the most familiar place, the most mundane task, can be a constant source of the new and unexplored.

Cultural anthropologist Jeff Salz says that most of us today are starved for adventure, but we can find all the adventure we need by being mindful and living fully in the moment. For Salz, the everyday challenges of being a father, husband, and businessman are more exciting than mountain climbing. He also brings insights from his mountain-climbing background to his understanding of mindfulness and work. He notes:

> If we're too focused on the summit we lose our footing and the joy of the process. In sustaining a career or spiritual path, there also has to be a constant focus on the moment, informed by a general direction, undertaken with the faith that the outcome will be positive. . . . Savoring the intrinsic pleasures of each moment turns out to be the most effective method for dealing with the vicissitudes of long-term change.[11]

Finding and Following Your Own Spiritual Journey

How shall you journey through your work and life? Only you and your soul can answer that. Hopefully the stories in this chapter will inspire your journey. But they, and the whole idea of a spiritual journey, may also be overwhelming. So relax. Pray. Give thanks for the ways you already see your work as a spiritual journey.

Take one step at a time toward a deeper union with your true self and with God through your work. Savor that step, and when you are ready, take another. Remember that all of the journeys presented here happened one step at a time, and many of those steps went sideways or backwards. Without those "mis-steps" — which must at times have seemed like failure or meaningless hardship — none of the stories here would have been nearly so rich.

3

Creating and Using
a Workplace Altar

A place where you feel inspired to do your best. A welcoming place where your heart lifts and your soul stretches. A place where you can serve purposefully, perhaps find kindred spirits. A place where you can laugh one moment, and contemplate the mysteries of life and the wonders of the universe the next.

Does this sound like your workplace? It could, at least some of the time, if you create and use well what I'll call a *workplace altar*.

Like other altars that have been created throughout the ages in every culture, workplace altars are a natural response to the need for respectful reflection wherever we are — at home, in a temple, in the woods, at work. Whether created spontaneously and designed to be temporary, or maintained over many lifetimes, altars invite us to humble ourselves, be still, and meet God.

Altars are frequently the focal points of sanctuaries (from the Latin word for "holy"). Here, the most important rituals are conducted. *Sanctuary* also means a place of refuge, such as a haven for quiet rest in the midst of noisy chaos, or a place of compassionate hospitality in the midst of danger and hostility.

For some people, Quakers for example, sacred space and sanctuary are created primarily through silence and dedicated simplicity. For others, for example, Hindus and many Christian communities, there is a formal altar containing objects that symbolize the community's unique dedication to

God. At times, the altar extends into a shrine, or collection of objects and art that celebrate devotion to a particular faith and inspire its practice.

As we will see later in this chapter, workplace altars may combine any of these elements in many forms. Whatever their form, however, workplace altars share some common intents. "Right here, right now," they invite, "enter the realm of the sacred and reconnect to the wonder of life. Discover here what is most essential—what sacrifices and commitments are needed, and what absolutely may not be relinquished in the name of work.

"Slow down and be still, so you can sink into the presence of God. Be quiet, so you can hear the wisdom you need to guide your life. Heal here. Strengthen your soul here. Be filled with new blessings. Go forth with new courage and peace."

Because of business needs and labor laws, workplace altars need to be discreet and designed to support—never impede—the purposes of your specific job. The underground workplace of Patsy Attwood, a station agent for the San Francisco Bay Area Rapid Transit System, is an example. You could walk by and never notice how beautifully her space integrates faith and work without displaying a single religious object.

Attwood works in a glass-walled booth in the midst of a noisy, artificially lit subway station. All day, she has to unlock jammed farecard machines and swing open or closed their heavy doors. The work is physically demanding and the setting offers absolutely no privacy. Yet, to Attwood, the space is the temple where she performs a ministry of blessing all who pass by.

Whenever Attwood enters or leaves her workspace, she blesses it. Whenever she glances at her phone console, a prayer she wrote reminds her to live her values moment to moment. On breaks, she reads her Bible and prays. Having been transferred recently to one of the system's busiest stations, where she works alone for several hours a day, she spends a lot of time on her knees during breaks praying for patience. And although relieving stress is not Attwood's primary motivation for praying while she works, stress naturally dissolves while she prays. Her spiritual practices also help her do a better job and leave her with plenty of energy after work for a fulfilling homelife.

Attwood tells of a big man who became infuriated when a farecard machine twenty feet from her booth failed to work. As he turned toward her with what she called an "eat-you-up attitude that made my stomach tremble like it does in an earthquake," she prayed, "God help me!" and meant it. By the time the angry customer reached her workspace, she felt as if she were surrounded by the arms of God.

Attwood patiently listened as the man berated the transit system and everyone who worked for it. When he finally ran out of breath, she smiled and said quietly, "I want to help you. Unfortunately, you spoke so fast I couldn't catch it all. Would you please tell me in fewer words and a quieter voice just what you need, so I can understand you better and help you get on your way."

Stunned, the man complied. After quickly solving the problem, Attwood wished the man well. The next day, the same man sought her out. "I don't know what you did to me," he said, "but the rest of my day was great."

How to Create Your Personal Workplace Altar

There are many simple ways to transform your workplace into a sanctuary that enlivens your soul. The following examples are from the Workplace Altars Project, a collection of stories and photos I began in 1996 as a project for San Francisco Bay Area Organizational Development Network's first meetings on spirituality and work.

A corporate attorney, starved for inspiration during long days, tucked a Bible and a book on Zen into his briefcase. Merely glancing at these books whenever he opened his briefcase encouraged him to take a deep breath, relax, and focus on working more purposefully. Gradually he found the courage to bring the books out of hiding and onto his desktop, where they became a part of an extensive library including the Koran, the Bhagavad Gita, and a dozen other texts. Brightly tabbed with Post-it Notes™ marking favorite passages, this man's workplace library became an ongoing source of wisdom and a catalyst for prayer.

Another attorney has created a sanctuary by replacing harsh florescent lighting with an antique desk lamp and floor lamps. A beautiful rug sets an inviting tone. Numerous plants help him stay more connected to nature, while little toys, such as a Minnie Mouse attached to the telephone console, add humor. The beauty and grace of the office help him work more efficiently and comfortably. This significantly increases the number of after-work hours he can devote to providing free legal service to AIDS and cancer patients.

A government fire safety trainer attached to the left of her computer a photograph of school children enjoying one of her talks. This photo of her satisfied "target market" keeps her focused on her purpose. While she works, she often prays for guidance on how best to convey to children information that could someday save their lives. Miniature Disney figures atop the computer help her remember to keep her message light so the children can receive it.

In each of these cases, sacred space was created by taking simple, prayerful actions based on individual needs and callings. Permission from corporate or government authorities was neither sought nor obtained. However, great care was taken—although often unconsciously—to blend the sacred space discreetly into the secular work environment.

This means that even if your faith calls you to witness to others at all times, witness at work through your kindness, your compassion, your sense of hospitality, your integrity. Do not preach or proselytize through your words or through anything you might place in your workspace. Otherwise, you invite legal action against your employer on such grounds as the "creation of a hostile atmosphere," and you may well be fired.

Workplace altar guidelines vary according to the setting. What you put in private space—your desk drawer, pocket, briefcase, or purse—is generally your own business. What you put in public space—ledges designed for the delivery and receipt of correspondence, the reception area, walls, and lunchroom or other common areas—is the employer's business. What you put in semi-private space—the visible sections of your desk or office that are obviously for your own use—is open to creative discretion. For example, having a small religious object on your computer monitor stand or in the bookcase facing you will probably be fine in your firm. However, positioning a symbol where it faces the public or other workers, especially if you are a supervisor, is not. Keeping religious tracts in your desk so you can read them on breaks is usually acceptable, but placing them by your outbox with a sign asking people to take them is not.

Many people say they have absolutely no problem with practicing their faith at work within guidelines like this. "I don't need a cross to remind me that I am a Christian," said one executive, "and I'm very sensitive to how people of other faiths might feel when they come into my office for an evaluation or other meeting. My essential challenge is to remember to make room for Christ in my life throughout my day. So I put a miniature chair next to a plant. Every time I see the chair, I remember my commitment to Christ. The only other person who knows what the chair means to me is a Jewish co-worker. She's my most important prayer partner at work."

Workplace altars in banks, HMOs, corporate offices, small businesses, and so on, display a lot of creativity and thought. Inspiring artwork and plants create a beautiful setting. Small desktop fountains or fish tanks help create an atmosphere of reflection. Inspirational books may be tucked among books needed for specific projects. Beautifully printed prayers or quotes may be taped onto computer monitor stands or placed in small frames where they can be seen throughout the day. Inspirational quotes may be placed in the appointment book or in files for difficult projects.

Pictures of loved ones or inspirational settings are common. So are rocks. A secretarial supervisor put on her desk three rocks from various retreats she attended. The rocks are like touchstones, she says, reminding her of the commitments she made or the insights she gained during those retreats.

Some workplace altars extend into the entire workspace. For example, a highly efficient executive secretary has filled his space with beautiful artwork, quotes, and a fountain. When he goes on breaks, others often sit in his space so they can be refreshed.

People on the go also have ways to stay connected with what matters to them. A fireman uses the inside of his locker door to post inspirational verses and pictures. A carpenter begins his day by blessing his tools and praying for his customers. A trainer awakes to a recording of her children's laughter, not an alarm, when she travels. A meter maid keeps devotional materials in her truck; on breaks, she pulls over to the side of the road and reads or prays. A factory worker goes into a storeroom during breaks, where she chants her religion's prayers.

The first time the Workplace Altars Project photos were shown, a young man I'll call Tom said that he stripped everything personal and enriching from his workspace after a co-worker, Joe, was laid off and escorted out of the building without being given time to retrieve his personal belongings or say good-bye to others. (This procedure is a common practice companies use to ensure that outgoing employees do not sabotage the company by manipulating or destroying computers or files.) Joe's personal photos and other desk items were supposed to be boxed up and mailed to him immediately. Boxed they were, but then they sat gathering dust for months, and Tom became so fixated on the possibility of being laid off that he turned his own workspace into a sterile station so that he would never have to suffer the indignity of having his things mistreated.

A drawing of Tom sitting in his sterile workspace with his eyes fixed on the neglected box labeled "Joe's stuff" is now part of the Workplace Altars Project. Often it invokes similar stories. It also invokes dialogue, such as this compilation of comments from members of a church adult education group: "Working in any job is like loving somebody. The relationship can end at any time. The question is, do you fixate on the possibility of loss, or do you give fully to the relationship now? If I were Tom, I'd explore whatever feelings are triggered by this incident. Then I'd bring back things into my workspace that feed my soul while I work, and I'd be prepared to lose them. I'd also be prepared to assert myself until my things were carefully returned to me."

Choosing the Right Material for Your Workplace Altar

In choosing materials for workplace altars, the essential spiritual guidelines are to bring into the space only those items that deepen or enhance your spiritual practices. It always helps to de-clutter your workspace and organize it in a fashion that works best for workspace and prayer space.

Next, through prayer, discover the specific spiritual issues that need your attention while you work. Then pray for guidance about the symbols and objects that will help you work with those issues. For example, during a very hard time when my stepmother, father-in-law, and brother-in-law were dying on the other side of the country, I posted pictures that reminded me of their love. Next to their pictures, I attached an encouraging poem a friend had given me.

During another hard time, when it seemed my vocational visions were moving further from fulfillment, I brought in a photo of Dr. Mary McLeod Bethune, a civil rights leader and educator whose life work inspires me.[1]

Creating a Group Workplace Altar

Creating a group workplace altar requires careful and hospitable attention to group sensibilities, for the symbols and practices that are sacred to one group may be anathema to another. One practice that works well is the creation of a group fountain, which can be made with a large, wide container, an aquarium pump with adjustable flow, and some clean rocks or shells. Most pumps now come with instructions on making fountains; most sellers of pumps can give you tips.

Before you actually create a fountain, however, test your pump in a kitchen or other area where you can wipe up spills without damaging wood or fabric finishes. Put the pump in the center of the container you have chosen, and place rocks loosely around it. Fill with plenty of water to cover the pump's intake hole, then plug in the pump. Adjust the flow until you get just the right amount of flow and sound without splashing water on the floor or tabletop.

Now you're ready to ritually position your group workplace altar. Empty out your rocks and water, then place the container and pump in its place of honor. Creating a fountain can then be a ceremony of commitment or team building. Each person can bring rocks from meaningful places. As people add a personal rock to the pile, they can speak what they bring to the group: their questions, concerns, best wishes.

If you want to add plants to your fountain, make sure they can live in water only, as dirt can clog the pump. Fountains, in fact, are great places to root plant cuttings, which can then be given away as a symbol of your group's values.

Sacred space can also be created with flowers. Fill your container with fresh baby's breath, to symbolize the invisible spirit or values of the group. Invite participants to select one flower from an assortment of as many different colors and types of flowers as possible. (Use silk flowers if anyone in the group is allergic to fresh ones. Also avoid strongly scented flowers in small spaces.) In turn, invite people to add a flower to the bouquet and make a statement of whatever joy, concern, and/or gift they bring to the table at that moment. Allow a little silence and space between each person's contribution.

Flowers are a perfect nonjudgmental, universal symbol of diversity, beauty, and abundance. Baby's breath, although delicate, can support heavier flowers, making it a great symbol of the invisible mysteries that support us all.

This flower ceremony is very adaptable. I first was introduced to it almost twenty years ago at Sevenoaks Pathwork Center in Madison, Virginia, where it was part of a welcoming ceremony. At the first gathering of the interfaith Oakland Coalition of Congregations in the early nineties, a representative of each congregation placed a flower into the vase after saying the name of the particular congregation followed by the commitment, "We are here to serve." Since then, it has been used in a variety of other settings. It works because it is as simple and powerful as lighting candles, and it creates a comfortable invitation for people to be authentic with one another.

Simplicity is a great basic guideline for any workplace altar. Don't be surprised if, after much prayer and reflection, you do little to change the outer form of your workspace. The most important thing is to treat your workspace as sacred space. Thus, whenever you enter this space, you can connect to the deepest truth within and outside yourself as you commit to serving the highest good. In this space, you can more easily take time to nurture your soul so that it can help you do whatever work you are paid — and called — to do.

4

Turning Stress and Burnout into Energy and Insight

Our natural stress release and burnout-prevention gifts begin with instincts that communicate basic messages like "I need sleep or food" or "I need to stop eating" or "I've got to get out of here. Now!" Heed these messages, and either stress disappears or we gain resources to handle a stressful situation.

We're also endowed with a resilient and compassionate core that can access intuition and many other sources of wisdom as easily as a tree's taproots can tap underground water during a drought. Plus, we are endowed with the gift of laughter, which by itself can lower blood pressure, enhance the immune system, deflate the ego, and disarm a bully.

By patiently developing these gifts and humbly seeking guidance, we can cut through information overload or conflicting advice. We then can generate energy and courage we didn't know we had and access wisdom sources much greater than ourselves.

The most powerful gifts come alive through challenge, as is beautifully illustrated in a photo taken in 1940 during the London Blitz by *Life* magazine photographer Robert Capa.[1]

Few situations are more stressful than the fifty-seven nights when Adolph Hitler (then the world's best-armed madman) ordered his air force to rain bombs on London all night long. His intent was to demoralize the British. Instead, his actions inspired the release of a powerful resilient spirit.

Every night during the Blitz, many Londoners took their suitcases into the Tube (subway), where they attempted to sleep. In the morning, they emerged from the Tube to discover if their homes or workplaces had survived. Then after another day of working under stressful situations, Londoners would again return to the Tube, where they sought enough sleep to meet the challenges of another day.

In the background of Capa's photo, friends converse, feet dangling, as they sit companionably atop uncomfortable-looking wooden bunks. At the base of one bunk, a man in a hard hat confers with an official. In the foreground, an elderly couple gaze adoringly at each other. In front of them are the remains of a shared meal and tea, perched atop a dirty, and probably smelly, oil drum. Around the couple is an aura of oasis. They, like everyone else in the photo, model an ability to thrive in uncertain and highly stressful situations. They also look blissful. Their faces speak of decades of loving, and of the choice to keep loving in spite of the fact that one or both of them would undoubtedly die within a few years, if not that very night.

I often show this photo to workshop participants without mentioning where or when it was taken. "Just from the body language and other cues, how stressed and burnt out do the people in this picture look to you?" I ask.

Typically, participants note that everyone except the elderly couple looks very tired, but less stressed than many of them feel after a hard day's work and commute. No one in the picture, they say, looks burnt out.

"The people in this picture remind me of the combination of courage and camaraderie we used to have in the hospital where I work," said a nurse. "Then, work was satisfying, even when it was difficult. Now we're harried and divided. When we try to discuss how burnt out we are, we're accused of being poor team players. But how can we create team spirit when we can't be honest about what's really going on?"

"I wish I could feel purposeful about my work like the people in the Blitz were," says an executive. "Too often I feel that no matter how hard I work, the results don't matter in the long run."

Another executive says, "I do love my work but I often burn out because I spend too much time being the one in charge. This picture reminds me that I need to spend more time relaxing with friends, like the people in the top bunks, or letting people I love know how much they matter to me, like that elderly couple."

Much wisdom for work-life excellence appears in this photo: stay focused on what matters. Deal as effectively as possible with what you are called to change; accept the rest. Use creativity and other gifts to take care of yourself while you follow your commitment to work well. Tend your relationships and allow others to support you.

Unfortunately, it's too easy to disconnect from our God-given wisdom sources and let stress build during busy days. Yet, it is during our busiest times that we most need divine guidance, for unchecked stress can lead to the spirit-sapping condition we call *burnout.*

Burnout is disorienting. We become like household pets who flee a firestorm, then can't find their way home because the smells which normally provide orienting cues have been replaced by signals that make no sense.

"The main causes of burnout are regretting the past, repressed creativity, and fear of the future," says Jim Conlon, a Catholic priest who directs the multidisciplinary and interfaith Sophia Center graduate program at Holy Names College in Oakland, California. When told the story of Capa's photo from the Blitz, Conlon could see immediately why the people exhibited no signs of burnout. "They are fully present. They are living joyfully and creatively. They are taking the risk to love and they are living the art of loving."[2]

Pride, Self-Will and Fear:
The Primary Barriers to Resilience

When we act at work like many Londoners did during the Blitz, we become experts in resilience. Rather than deny problems or wait for someone to rescue us, we utilize core gifts such as perspective, creativity, and our drives to excellence and self-expression. At the same time, we welcome the support of others and the grace of God. In the process, we grow. Thus, we can bounce or spring back from problems that initially may weaken or dis-spirit us.

To create resilience, we first have to be willing to see reality as it is. Then we need to give our best to the challenge while accepting the fact that we can't control the outcome. Three basic negative human tendencies prohibit us from doing all this by distorting or blocking our natural gifts and positive tendencies. These negative tendencies, or faults, are pride, self-will and fear.[3]

Pride: Many kinds of *pride* flourish at work. Arrogance, vanity, and self-absorption are among the best known. One way these forms of pride contribute to stress and burnout is by driving us to measure ourselves by distorted standards. Thus, rather than ask ourselves, "What course of action will be most effective and meaningful?" we ask (often unconsciously), "What course of action will make me look better than others?" Or, as Scarlett O'Hara, the selfish heroine of Margaret Mitchell's popular novel, *Gone with the Wind*, might put it, "What course of action will make the most people feel pea-green with envy?"

Masking more blatant forms of pride are idealized self-images. Many of these have been repeated so often that they sound like mantras: "I'm tough." "I don't need anybody." "I can work 24-7." "I'm so loyal to this firm that I missed the births of all four of my children."

An idealized image of "I'm decisive!" can be very expensive to individuals and companies, because our culture practically deifies the image of the decisive leader and we tend to treat dissenting viewpoints as disloyal. Rather than humble ourselves and admit, "I don't know, but I wish to learn," rather than invite insight from many directions or be willing to enter the dark nights of the soul, we intensify stressful problems by acting too quickly on limited information.

Self-will: Self-will comes from the part in us that says, "No, God, I don't want your kingdom. I don't want your rules. I want my own way, and I want it right now!" One form of self-will comes from free will gone awry. Rather than balance our drives for self-assertion and self-expression with compassion and discernment, we insist upon our way of seeing and doing things. We become obsessed with winning or power.

An equally destructive form of self-will comes from the repression of healthy free will. Jake, a bright young man who dreams of a creative job, isn't willing to give up the negative pleasures he gets from his exhausting and poorly paid bureaucratic position under bosses he deems inferior. So long as Jake stays in this job, he enjoys commiserating with others who also lack the courage to discover or follow their own creative dreams. With them, he gets to act smug and engage in the "whose boss is the worst?" contests. He also enjoys the opportunity to feel superior to his bosses and, at least temporarily, forget his perpetual feelings of insecurity. These negative pleasures, he tells himself, outweigh his exhaustion and lack of fulfillment at work.

Fear: Fear as a fault is a distorted perception of danger that has been projected by pride or self-will. To the extent that we are invested in a prideful self-image (whether an image of power or serenity or anything else), we feel threatened by any hints that we are not living up to those images. Thus, we worry that others might unmask our imperfections. To the extent that we are invested with having our own way (or impeding the power of others to have their way), we feel threatened by any barriers to the fulfillment of our desires.

Genuine fear, on the other hand, is a message from such divine gifts as instinct and intuition. In 1989, during what later became known as the Loma Prieta earthquake, for instance, I experienced sharp bristling feelings running up and down my spine seconds before my conscious mind registered, "Earthquake! Big one! Take cover!" Almost instantly, thanks to a surge of adrenaline and heightened awareness, I surveyed the scene and got easily under a desk, in spite of two normally painful knee injuries.

Fear is always worth exploring, says therapist Bill Say. "If we are afraid of fear or unconscious of it, we are paralyzed by it or driven by it."[4]

A good example of this occurred while I was working on a project in a small firm headed by Joe, a willful and perfectionistic micromanager. For months Joe had driven the staff with his inflated notions of all that had to be done within a certain time frame in order to get a specific job done well. Whenever staff had complained about overwork and wondered if the client was really being served well by the firm's increasingly expensive service, Joe had humiliated them into working harder.

As a temp who had been called in to help out for a few weeks, I was assigned to help Joe's sister, whose office in another state was usually insulated from Joe's outbursts. Then came a day of many deadlines, and Joe became so rushed that he failed to give clear instructions for his many demands. This meant some things didn't get done, some things were done twice, and many things were done wrong.

Tempers quickly flared between Joe and his sister. Problems in our office escalated with simple things like carelessly refilled copier trays creating paper jams. Important papers were misplaced, resulting in more confusion and wasted time, more frayed tempers.

To regain my lost efficiency, I went to the only quiet place around, the restroom, and prayed for guidance. Immediately, an image of two dragons appeared. The one with the fiery breath promoted obsessive activity by saying repeatedly, "More! You've got to do more!" The other halted activity through his icy, paralyzing breath and the words, "You've got to be careful, because everything you do could be wrong."

These symbolic dragons thrive throughout the business and nonprofit world. Being caught in their spell is as exhausting and ineffective as it is to drive down a road in full throttle with all the brakes on. Breaking the dragons' spell, however, is as simple and as difficult as accepting the truth of their words. Yes, there is always more we can do, and yes, anything we do can be wrong. Only when we accept this basic truth can we have the humility and courage to know and do our best.

Spiritual Disciplines:
The Antidote to Pride, Self-Will, and Fear

Andre Delbecq, a professor at Santa Clara University, conducts courses on spirituality and leadership that attract executives and MBA students throughout California's Silicon Valley. There is, he says, "a deep yearning to attach meaning to work, and business empowers people to pour themselves into service."

Delbecq quotes Psalm 139 as an expression of the universal longing to be who we were in the mystery of creation, when God held us and called us by name. "When I am myself," he said, "I can commit to love. I can spill myself and my creativity in service. Business solutions then can come from creativity, not from a script."

Delbecq's students already know the importance of time and self-management in order to maintain perspective. His classes help students see how spiritual disciplines are like "white space"[5] that allows them to "enter into greater awareness and develop diversity of values." For executives, the favored form of contemplative practices are those that allow them to unplug their senses.[6]

Delbecq notes that spiritual disciplines also help us

... avoid the seductions of hubris and greed, as well as the idolatry of speed. The "first mover advantage" is considered so important, especially in the high-tech industry, that caution is often sacrificed. The problem is compounded by greed. Greed says we don't have time to figure it out, to reflect.[7]

Because fear so often underlies or magnifies greed and other spirit-crippling forms of pride and self-will, one of the most humbling and courageous spiritual practices is to face fear. This requires letting go of the spiritual arrogance that says, "I have it all together" and any demand that, "Because I'm spiritual, God should protect me from all harm."

Therapist Bill Say counsels, "Rather than prop yourself up against fear, it's better to flow into it, process it, and let it take you into wonderful places."[8] One of those wonderful places is the renewed faith that, in spite of our faults, we are always worthy of love and compassion. No matter how hard our challenge, we don't have to face it alone. Even if we face death of the physical body, that is not the end of our spiritual life.

When we face the truth, our scary dragons melt, for they are nothing but projections of our fear, pride, or self-will. In their place is a pure spring. To benefit from its healing and guiding powers, all we need to do is kneel before that spring and pray, "God, I want to give my best in this task. Help me see clearly my next step. Help me follow your will."

Many spiritual teachers unwittingly impede our ability to learn from fear. Dispatch all fear and doubt right away, some suggest, as if it were like a deadly e-mail virus that could destroy all faith if it were opened and examined. Others say fear isn't real, just fictional events appearing real. Yet, when we dare look at fear with an open heart and discerning eye, here are a few of the important messages that it can deliver:

- *Hunches* that someone is untrustworthy or that some action is unethical. When we heed these hunches, we gain an opportunity to clarify a misperception or to stop a small ethical lapse from turning into one that could seriously damage ourselves and others.

- *"Butterflies"* that come from being at our growing edge. Pay attention to these butterflies, and we may discover a need for increased support or attentiveness. Or the butterflies may just signal blocked excitement and pleasure.
- *Fault lines,* or the deep cracks in our souls where pride and self-will keep us from knowing and seeing God's will. Whenever we try to build our lives and work atop these fault lines, we will always feel fearful, for whatever we build there will be vulnerable to our personal equivalent of earthquakes.
- *Vulnerability,* or the awareness of what it always means to be human and know that inevitably we will die and that we depend on love from fellow humans who fear love and life as much as we do.

To be human today is to be vulnerable to economic and political upheaval that is throwing many of us out of work and shattering the foundations of how we do business. It takes courage to let another see how vulnerable we feel. "I need you to listen to how scary my life feels right now," a friend said recently. "Don't try to fix me, because if you do, I won't be able to trust you with the deepest parts of myself, the parts I don't yet know how to describe. So please, just listen."

It is hard to listen like this, however, for without solutions in sight, new depths of vulnerability may be revealed in speaker and listener. But in the depths of shared vulnerability there are forged new depths of wisdom and trust. This is precisely the kind of foundation we need if we are to build a new economy that works for us all.

"Just Walk through It and Have Faith"

All the practices that are mentioned throughout this book can help alleviate stress and prevent or heal burnout. A workplace altar can help you anchor into what matters most and remind you to pray through hard times. Taking time to reflect on all the people your work impacts can help you remember the many ways you can express your gratitude and gifts into the world. Seeing your momentary challenges in the context of a larger spiritual journey may help you see more meaning in the moment and discover new allies or internal resources.

Much of my most exciting work today came out of a hard period between 1990 and 1995 when my work vision wasn't yet clear or grounded (though I thought it was) and when my husband, John, was out of work a lot. The guidance that came from prayer at this time seemed contradictory: keep working to develop ideas from my master's thesis about how people reclaim and develop their visionary potentials; get a full-time job as a legal secretary in order to earn a good living while leaving my energy and mind free after the workday was over. That guidance also kept saying, "This is one of those dark nights of the soul. Just walk through it and have faith."

Not long after I took a full-time job as a floating legal secretary in a very large law firm—which meant I worked for whomever needed me at the time—John's dad had a stroke and my stepmother, Violet, who had been a beloved part of our family since I was sixteen, was diagnosed with colon cancer. After a year or so of doing as much overtime as possible so we could afford to fly across country to be with our parents, our cat, Sushi, was diagnosed with kidney failure. Soon after that, we got word that John's brother-in-law had liver cancer.

For months, John and I sat together in the kitchen each evening, holding Sushi and crying as we dripped fluids under the skin of our dear trembling cat. We cried for Sushi, who rallied for a while, then slowly faded away. We cried for our own fragility, and we cried for the family members we could not hold nearly so often as we would have liked.

Sometimes, the only motivation for going to work I could feel was, "I have to keep working so we can afford more trips back East and see people we love before they die" or "I have to stay efficient enough not to be caught in the next round of downsizing." It made a huge difference during that time to remember the guidance, "This is one of those dark nights of the soul. Just walk through it and have faith."

Desperation made me discover that the firm was filled with kindred spirits, including Sara Cox. She always had a moment for a quick hug and a listening ear behind a closed door. Once she gave me an inspirational Rilke poem, which I put up in my workspace and read often.

I never got from Sara, "You can sit and weep here for hours and I'll console you," because both of us had jobs to do. But it only takes a moment of real attention to make a big difference. Buoyed by contact with people like Sara, I learned to make more meaningful moments for myself. While waiting on hold on the telephone or standing at the copier, I'd practice simple breathing and focusing exercises. Deep breath in, thinking "Thank you, God"; deep breath out, thinking "Help me, God."

The fruits of the work I hadn't consciously chosen during that hard time are many. Our marriage and family relationships strengthened. My work vision became much more grounded and integrated. Frustrated with my inability to build "spiritual work" as fast as I wished, I began seeing spiritual work all around me in workplace altars. Although I would not realize it by the time I left the firm with a small stake for building my business vision, the experience had begun to reveal to me the heart and soul of law, as well as some part I might play in helping to heal that soul.

Tools for Bringing Spirit to Workday Challenges

The following tools and visualization exercises may help you increase meaning and joy in your work while you release stress and prevent burnout.

Ask questions and allow your entire body, mind, and spirit to offer answers. The questions, "What can I learn in this situation about my faults, my gifts, and my true needs?" and "How can I serve here?" are always helpful. Sometimes inner guidance comes back as simple as, "Be more attentive" or "Commit more to doing well the job you are being paid to do" or "Be grateful for your work. Bless it; bless yourself; bless everyone around you." At other times, questions lead to more questions that need to be explored with a trusted friend over a lunch break or taken to prayer after work.

An important way to prevent stress from building into burnout is to pay attention to your body while you work. Notice your breathing patterns and how they affect your energy and emotions. Notice the differences between how you hold your body when you are under stress as opposed to when you are relaxed. Notice the particular ways you react to stress.

For example, do you collapse in the chest, which forces your arms to dangle limply and your head to droop, so you see fewer options and your energy level drops? If so, sit more erect so each vertebra can help support the one above, and your lungs have room to expand fully. Take some slow, deep breaths as you make a few swimming movements. Notice how this gives you increased energy, and a little more faith in your ability to endure specific challenges.

Humor and imagination are great stress and burnout-busters that you can use at any time. Humor breaks tension as it lightens the spirit. Imagination helps your mind and soul shake loose debilitating patterns and create more effective ones. The following suggestions are some visualizations I invented or adapted that you may find useful.

Turn your problems into a comedy. Picture your day through the eyes of a master comedian like Whoopi Goldberg. Imagine all the great material she could find from your commute, your demanding family or boss, your overloaded desk, etc.

If you feel like having a pity party, have a really great one in your mind. Imagine fantastic costumes for your tormentors, like those in Batman movies. After you've had your laugh, take a deep breath and look at your problems afresh.

Imagine having a brain cleaning. Imagine how your brain looks when it's tired. For example, instead of a healthy organism, you see a foggy cavern filled with dust and cobwebs. Your computer circuits are blown, your nerves frayed. Sparks fly, creating short circuits.

Now imagine an army of skilled helpers repairing your mental wiring and circuits. They ensure that your memory banks work well again, and that everything is clearly labeled. They check all your network connections, so you can access information freely again.

Meanwhile, other helpers vacuum and scrub your brain until it hums. They polish your mental desktops and file away your worries in well-marked cabinets. Others flush your tired eyes with cool spring water, oil your joints, and massage your tired muscles.

You can enhance this fantasy by closing your eyes and letting them enjoy the darkness for a moment or two, or by doing some simple physical exercises like shrugging your shoulders or blinking your eyes rapidly for two minutes to break the muscular tension at the back of the head.

Consult the wise one. Imagine walking down a path in a beautiful forest. Even if the terrain is new to you, imagine knowing you are safe. Feel how your step is sure and excited.

Deep in the forest, you come to a clearing. There, in a lovely small building, a spiritual teacher welcomes you.

Ask any questions that puzzle you. Listen to the wise one's answers. Before you leave, the wise one gives you a blessing, such as a stone, a flower, words of inspiration, and/or a healing touch. The wise one then gives you instructions on how to summon him or her again whenever you need additional guidance.

Finally, give thanks, say good-bye, walk back down the path through the woods, and return to your normal life with renewed insight.

This visualization is a wonderful prelude to prayer or meditation. Variations of it have been used in many traditions.

Walk your meditation practices into the world. Begin with any meditation practice that helps you become centered and focused. Maintain the practice while walking. Some variations to try:

- Silently repeat a prayer or affirmation while you walk, such as, "I welcome divine guidance."
- Select one hand to represent meaning and joy, and the other to represent your work. Let them roll into each other so each one has its beginning in the other and each one supports the other. As you walk, feel the support for your hands (and, by extension, meaning, joy, and work) from your heart, your breath, your legs, etc. Ask for guidance on how each part of you can support meaning and joy through your work.
- Bless everyone and everything you see while you walk. As you breathe out, send out your goodwill; as you breathe in, give a prayer of gratitude.

Carry spiritual wisdom with you at all times. In addition to the written word that you may carry in your pocket or tuck into your desk, why not memorize your favorite psalm or other verses of Scripture? By memorizing and bringing to mind brief inspirational sayings, wisdom will be with you always, ready to heal your wounded soul, then generate the energy and insight you need for meaningful and satisfying work.

5

Finding Wisdom for Work from Many Traditions

Some time in the late fifties, Grandmother decided it was time for another warning about people who are different from us. About pagans and heathens, she said little. Even if by some remote chance I did happen to meet any, she trusted that I would be too horrified by their strange ways to be led astray by their teachings.

Grandmother was very worried, however, that I might come under the spell of Catholics. Not only had she grown up with warnings against Catholics (as well as Jews and even Episcopalians), she had also visited a Catholic mission as a tourist. There she had seen something so horrifying that she could hardly imagine its import as she whispered her accusation, "They mumble over beads."[1]

Grandmother's concern was not unusual or mean-spirited. Indeed, the parents of the Catholic boy I had met on a camping trip were worried that he liked me, a Protestant. In warning us to stick to our own kind, our elders were following a time-honored, worldwide tradition. Thus were prejudices and misunderstandings maintained and even intensified.

Once it was assumed that, at work, we would be protected from contact with others from different traditions. Now, labor laws and cultural shifts at work bring us together — gay beside straight, devout believer beside unaffiliated groper[2] or committed eclectic.

Thus, at work today, we cannot avoid encountering people we've been carefully taught to hate or fear, and vice versa. People whose faith is guided by written scriptures may fear those whose primary teachers are earth and its creatures.

People who happily sing their faith don't know what to make of people whose primary practice is silence. People whose faith is eclectic brand often as narrow those who are obedient to only one way.

To learn to work well together, we have to cast off the blinders and distorting lens of prejudice, no matter how lovingly those prejudices were taught and learned. We have to give others the courtesy of discovering who they are—not who we fear they are or wish them to be.

According to cultural anthropologist Jeff Salz, work itself is a powerful common ground for finding meaning and creating justice in a diverse world. When he toured South America asking people about the meaning of life, overwhelmingly they said, "*trabajo*," or "work." Salz, however, did not understand this fully until he learned a basic Buddhist concept. "The Buddha said we don't work just to meet the needs of ourselves and others. We also work to move out of our preconceptions or isolation and into the world."[3]

The Wisdom of Tribal Traditions

When we bless others who are different from us by seeing them fully with unclouded eyes, we see a treasure trove of wisdom for work in all the world's religions. This treasure trove begins with tribal people, such as Australian aborigines or African tribes, whose wisdom has been handed down in small groups for hundreds of centuries. Common to tribal (also called *primal*, as in "first") people throughout the world is an ethic in which all work is enfolded into community and spiritual life. Long before there was literature, work tools were blessed and work was infused with ritual and prayer. Because work in tribal settings meets an obvious community need (including the need for beauty), its meaning is readily apparent.

Primal peoples' lives and spiritual practices are connected to the earth. There is awe and respect for the land which brings forth crops, and for animals who become food, teachers, clothing, and sometimes housing. Each turning of the season is celebrated. The earth and its inhabitants are expected to be protected, as in the Iroquois commandment to consider the impact of one's actions to the seventh generation.

Since the 1960s, interest in primal traditions, particularly Native American spirituality, has become widespread. For example, this has popularized drumming as a way to pray with the body and to attune a community to one heartbeat. Various purification rituals, particularly sweat lodges, offer participants from many religions an opportunity to experience a kind of confession and healing of the entire body, mind, and spirit. For these sweat lodges, a group of people ritually heat rocks, then carry those rocks into an enclosed, dark place and pour water on them.

As participants sweat in the darkness, they pray and chant. My husband, John, who has participated in four sweat lodges, says, "The feeling of being cleansed and renewed was not so much from anything extraordinary happening, but the experience of renewal, of letting go and clearing the mind and heart. It's a preparation and dedication to whatever task is coming up in the future."

There is a deceptive simplicity to the sweat lodge and other practices, however. It takes little time to learn the mechanics, but it takes years to develop spiritual mastery. After attending several sweat lodges, one young man decided that he was ready to conduct them. When he asked an elder for some pointers, the elder said, "You are welcome to come help us heat rocks for a couple of years, then we can see if you are ready for the next step." The young man wasn't interested.

Many Native American elders and leaders in other religions worry that their traditions are being co-opted or denigrated. These and other elders also welcome new appreciation for their viewpoints and teachings.

To what extent should you adapt or be inspired by other traditions? That is an ongoing question for prayer

and dialogue. Here are a few suggestions for some elements
of tribal traditions which may inspire you to deepen and
broaden your own faith tradition:

- a sense of humor combined with pragmatism
- a deep and abiding respect for nature and our divine
  command not to exploit it
- a habit of spending time alone in wilderness and discovering our kinship with *mitakue oyasin*, the Lakota
  (Sioux) words for "all my relations," human and otherwise

The Wisdom of World Religions

Many theologians from major religions worry about mixing
traditions, or *syncretism*. In *Shopping for Faith: American Religion in the New Millennium, Religion Watch* editor-publisher
Richard Cimino and *San Francisco Chronicle* religion editor
Don Lattin define syncretism as the "tendency to mix elements of different traditions into new hybrid forms." This
tendency, they predict, will "continue in the new millennium,
as seekers separated from their religious heritage search out
new expressions of faith."4 It will also continue in mainline
faith communities of all religions, as they seek to make their
practices more relevant to today's work and life realities.[5]

A common complaint among some religious leaders is
that the ecumenical spirit has led to a shallow or "salad bar"
approach to religion. But sometimes a salad is the most nur-
turing and appropriate meal. Sometimes the practices that
allow one to drink from the deep well of one's own traditions need to be enriched by surface explorations that allow
us to drink from the wells of other traditions.

Each world religion offers insights to inspire and challenge your thinking about spirit and work. Although this
book cannot possibly provide a comprehensive introduction
to all of them, the following unofficial insights from major
traditions may inspire you to explore further.

Hinduism: Hinduism is the oldest of today's major religions. It began about four thousand years ago in India. Unlike the three western religions of Judaism, Christianity and Islam, it does not have a "single founder, specific theological system, a single system or morality, or a central religious organization."[6] As such, it is confusing to many westerners, for it is neither as monotheistic nor polytheistic as it appears. Instead, some call it "henotheistic," in that there is only one supreme being, Brahman, who simultaneously transcends the universe and is at one with it.[7] At the same time, there is a variety of exotic gods and goddesses, from the elephant-headed Ganesh to the blue-faced, flute-playing Krishna, who represent different facets of this one supreme being.

Two Hindu beliefs that have become widely known over the past few decades are reincarnation and karma. *Reincarnation* refers to the belief that after death, the soul takes another body, so that it may learn new lessons. *Karma* is like the law of cause and effect, so that the condition of one's new life depends on the good or evil that was done in a previous life.

A few of the most important Hindu texts include: 1) the almost thirty-five-hundred-year-old Vedas, filled with hymns, prayers, and rituals; 2) the Upanishads, from between 800 B.C.E. and 400 B.C.E., which "elaborate on how the soul (Atman) can be united with the ultimate truth (Brahman) through contemplation and meditation, as well as the doctrine of Karma"[8]; and 3) the Bhagavad Gita, a long poetic conversation between Krishna and the warrior Arjuna.

A basic Hindu practice is yoga, which can be translated as "Pathway to God." Westerners typically are most familiar with Hatha Yoga, which is taught in schools and community centers everywhere as a way to relive stress, relax, and increase physical health. Like all other forms of Yoga, this practice has a spiritual basis: to strengthen and purify the physical house of the spirit.

In his work titled *A Sourcebook for Earth's Community of Religions*[9], editor Joel Beversluis lists four other forms of yoga:

- Bhakti Yoga is the way of devotion to personalized manifestations of God;
- Karma Yoga, the way of selfless service, is for persons with an inclination to be active with interpersonal concerns and obligations;
- Jnana Yoga names the path to God-realization through knowledge, and is particularly attractive for aspirants with a strong intellectual inclination;
- Raja Yoga, the path of meditation, is for those who choose an experimental and experiential approach.

Work as yoga calls us to work not from our ego, which builds a wall between us and God, but from our soul—which means working thoughtfully and serving everyone joyfully, as if we were serving God.

Hinduism sanctions pleasure and success in work, says Huston Smith, for "the world is awash with beauty and heavy with sensual delights. . . . India grants not only that success is a requisite for supporting a household and discharging one's civic responsibilities, but that its achievements confer dignity and self-respect. In the end, however, these rewards . . . harbor limitations."[10] Hence, Hinduism calls us to anchor not in self-centeredness or material rewards, but in practices that draw us closer to union with God.

One Hindu concept that many Westerners find difficult to understand is *nonattachment*, which can seem uncaring. But the true meaning of nonattachment is a willingness to relinquish the results of any action to God. Krishan Khalra, CEO of Biogenex in San Ramon, California, said that "attachment and fear of failure really create all the stress."[11] By studying the Hindu scriptures, the Bhagavad-Gita, he learned how to work hard and enjoy it, then switch off from work at the end of the day and enjoy quality family time.

Taoism: The origins of Taoism are not known exactly, although it is attributed to seventh-century B.C.E. Chinese philosopher Lao Tzu. *Tao* means "the way" for working within a mysterious universe. Balance is achieved by a union of opposites, which is symbolized by the yin-yang symbol in which two elements of equal size (but contrasting colors) flow into each other. In the heart of each element is a dot of the opposite color which represents the other.

The basic Taoist text, the *Tao Te Ching*, consists of eighty-one verses with commentary that are reputed to be Lao Tzu's teachings as recorded by a gatekeeper or written by Lao Tzu on his last day on earth. Their guidance for leading without forcing was popularized in the '60s as "Go with the flow," but the faith has much more depth than this brief phrase suggests.

A primary concept of Taoism is Wu-Wei or "not doing." This does not excuse laziness, but calls us to allow our being and acting (doing) to become one. Then, out of being, we do.

In Taoism, says John Mabry, author of *God as Nature Sees God: A Christian Reading of the* Tao Te Ching,[12]

> . . . the chief sin is forcing. The goal is to respond humanly, to be ourselves. If the natural response to an event is anger, the sage shows anger. The sage doesn't "second guess" her own feelings or those of others. She allows goodness to come naturally.
>
> The Tao says practice "not doing and nothing will remain undone" because when we do not force, the work is done without effort and as naturally as taking a nap by a stream. You commit to your work by taking your place, and eliminating the artificial boundary between you and the work. You become the work; the work becomes you. You allow yourself to fully enter into the work, and you flow with it.[13]

Judaism: Judaism traces its origins to a covenant between God and Abraham around 1800 B.C.E. The concept of *covenant,* or solemn and divine contract, is central to the Hebrew tradition with its emphasis on justice and integrity in all dealings. Out of these teachings came much of the heart and soul of the Western legal system.

From the Jewish ceremony of Simchat Torah, or "Rejoicing in the Law," comes a vision for how the best in human law could be developed and honored. Simchat Torah honors the yearly process of unscrolling and reading aloud a section of the Torah (the first five books of the Bible) a few selections at a time. At Simchat Torah, the community has completed reading the entire Torah. Now it is ready to rewind the Torah scroll and begin the unscrolling and reading cycle anew. But first, according to Merle Feld, author of *A Spiritual Life,* it is time for Simchat Torah, a joyous, raucous celebration of the Torah as a "holy code of behavior for living ethically, meaningfully and consciously."

Feld says that the ceremony invites our innocent and fun-loving child to dance with our serious self. "We've just experienced this extraordinary odyssey of self-reflection, fasting, self-examination [Yom Kippur or Day of Atonement]. We've started over and lived in the garden again [the harvest festival of Sukkot]. Simchat Torah affirms that we live in a world full of meaning. In that context we have a whole network of responsibilities for ourselves, for our families, for each other."[14]

From Judaism, in fact, comes the concept of *stewardship,* or the duty to care for the earth. This extends to Tikkun Olam, or the duty to do one's part to help others heal and to repair the world.

One of the most relevant tenets of Judaism to workers of all faiths is the Sabbath, which commands resting one full day out of seven. "The Sabbath is the antithesis of 24-7 work-days," says attorney-mediator Stewart Levine, author of *Getting to Resolution: Turning Conflict into Collaboration* (Berret-Koehler, 1998). "You dare to go off-line for reverie, for deep acknowledgement, for something other than forge-onward activities."[15]

Although it is difficult to find sabbath time in a wired-up world, August Turak, CEO of the Raleigh Group International software company, manages to do just that. When he works, Turak works hard and enjoys it. But he refuses to carry a cellphone after hours, and he doesn't work on a laptop during plane trips. He also retreats regularly to a Trappist monastery.[16]

Author Huston Smith successfully combines scholarship with humor. "What would it be like," he says about the Sabbath, "if God had gotten through the sixth day and said, 'This is good stuff' and kept going? We would have a surfeit of stuff, but God knew enough to stop. If we are made in the image of God, we should follow his example."[17]

Buddhism: Buddhism dates back to 500 B.C.E, after the enlightenment of Siddhartha, a wealthy prince who relinquished his wordly status. Buddhism has become popular because of its teachings on right livelihood and its meditation practices, including the concept of mindfulness, or being very present and attentive to what is happening here and now.

Buddhism promotes universal values such as loving kindness, compassion, appreciative joy, equanimity, and self-acceptance. World religions scholar Huston Smith, during a July 1998 interview, noted that there are major differences between Southern (Theravada) Buddhism and the Northern (Mayahana) branch. "Theravada society is divided into three segments—the government, the laity, and the monks," he said. "The work of the monks, like monastics in the West, is to cultivate the spirit and to let its resources help the laity. The monks work very hard. They get up very early and pray, but it is different from the work of the laity who support them.

"Many in the secular world often think monastics don't work, that monks are freeloaders because society supports them. Their work is actually the most important, but it is not making furniture, not building houses, not secular work.

"In Mayahana Buddhism, there is a Zen saying that 'one day of no working is one day of no eating.' Meaning, unlike the Theravadans, they try not to be beholden to society. When

I spent my time in a Zen monastery, I spent as much time working in the vegetable garden as in Zazen or meditation."

Zen Buddhism is now popular with executives, lawyers, and others who fear they have to always know the answer. Zen requires the constant cultivation of beginner's mind, for "in the beginner's mind there are many possibilities, but in the expert's there are few," says Zen Buddhist master Shunryu Suzuki.[18]

A basic Buddhist concept is the call to Right Livelihood. In a September 1996 article for *Conscious Choice* magazine, Chicago artist and writer Bobbye Middendorf wrote that right livelihood has "become a code in contemporary circles for earning one's daily bread out of doing work that is 'right.'" But what does right livelihood really mean, and how does one achieve it?

In search of an answer, Middendorf surveyed the literature in the career counseling field, and she interviewed numerous Buddhist practitioners and career counselors. The most comprehensive and clear answer she found came from career counselor Marti Beddoe, who said:

> *Right Livelihood* means to avoid any life that brings shame. It embodies the other seven steps along the eightfold path to enlightenment: Right Thought involves love and devotion through work. Right Mindfulness means consciously choosing your path and your work. Right Understanding evolved from consciously choosing work that is the best of ourselves and having knowledge of our values. Right Speech implies compassion relating to others through our work. Right Concentration means doing work with care and intense awareness and love. Right Action implies doing your work and having no attachment to the results. Right Effort is about choosing work you can do a whole life, keeping yourself in a state of constant learning and beginner's mind. The bottom line is this: Work that embodies love, devotion, and service is as much an attitude as the actions we take.[19]

Buddhist author Sandy Boucher offers guidance on what can happen when we commit fully to work and are willing to relinquish to God the results. Although she was speaking to writers, her wisdom applies to all work. Here she comments about the fear of finishing:

> When we complete a piece, we are fully committed to it. We have done the best we could, and there it is — ready to go out in the world with our name on it . . . And we will have no control over how it will be received.
>
> Someone may not like it. Another may like it for all the wrong reasons. . . . And we may have to look squarely at our strengths and limitations, for a completed piece is never perfect. While the [work] as a whole may succeed, we know the small failures embedded in it, the places where we just couldn't go far enough or reach deep enough. Finishing brings us up against our own imperfections, with no excuses now.
>
> But isn't that what life does anyhow? We can't really know what a relationship, a job, a project will be like until we give ourselves to it, meet its demand, fail or succeed, as we carry it through to its completion. In the process, we learn about ourselves. Some things we'll like, some we won't.[20]

Christianity: Christianity evolved in Israel about two thousand years ago with the life, teachings, death, and resurrection of Jesus. It is built on simple and magnificent stories that have changed dramatically the lives of people who have heard the power and wisdom of these stories.

Believers say that Jesus' birth fulfilled the centuries-old promise that one day a redeemer would be born into the Jewish house of David. With the birth of Jesus, God's only begotten Son was born, and was then raised to manhood by his virgin mother Mary and her husband, the carpenter Joseph. From the accounts of his birth in a stable to his painful crucifixion and glorious resurrection, the stories of

Jesus tell of one who spoke only compassionate truth in a manner that anyone could understand.

All religions offer guidance on how to deal with emptiness, pain, loss, grief, and death. For Christians, the symbol of the cross is a constant reminder that death is not the end of life. There is always the possibility of resurrection, which is available to all believers.

From the parables of Jesus comes the picture of a realist who appreciates the value of a widow's mite and an absolutely unhypocritical teacher who values a tiny thing given in love far more than a huge thing given without love. These parables also show an intimate relationship with the created world in their references to everything from grains of mustard to lilies of the field, and in their warnings to build on solid ground yet sow on loose and fertile soil.

In Jesus' name, his followers have healed the sick, cast out demons, and added their own eloquent calls to faith and goodness. Inspired by his willingness to sacrifice himself for the sake of others, they have braved persecution in a way that spread new faith. Some of the most powerful followers, including Paul (Saul) of Tarsus, had originally been skeptics or even determined to quash the new faith.

Acccording to Huston Smith, followers like Paul gave traction to the spirit of Jesus. "If Jesus hadn't been followed by Paul," Smith said during a July 1999 talk at the Sophia Center of Holy Names College, the eloquent "Sermon on the Mount would have floated into the ethers in two generations."

But as the stories of Jesus and his followers were written down and the Christian Church developed, controversy arose about whether or not these stories were the literal truth. Was Jesus actually the only begotten Son of God who, for a time, walked among us, then ascended to the right hand of God the Father, as many believe? Was he the promised Messiah long sought by the Jews? Or is Jesus a symbol for a mystery that calls us to see God not as remote from us, but within and all around us?

Whatever one's theological interpretations of Christian teachings, the life of Jesus naturally inspires dialogue and inspiration for everyday work and life. For example, how would Jesus suggest you deal with a lying boss or co-worker? What would he suggest you do on those days when you feel too brokenhearted to get up out of bed, much less go to work? How would he help you discern which of several choices is ethical?

One way to begin seeking answers for questions like these is to recall Jesus' basic attributes. Thus, if we seek to deal with a lying boss or co-worker, in the same way Jesus would, we know that our actions must be ethical, merciful, and compassionate, even when we are holding another accountable for his or her transgressions. We know that we must begin by seeking divine guidance and by being willing to follow that guidance, no matter how difficult. Like Jesus, we won't ask any special favors that aren't available to any other human, yet we will be prepared to help create something miraculous. And we will be open to receiving help from others, for Jesus also knew how to cherish his friends and take a good break. Although the Gospels are not explicit on this point, we'll almost surely need to temper our sense of dedication with a very healthy sense of humor.

Within the wide tent of Christianity today, there is a diverse array of denominations with a multiplicity of beliefs and practices. Some (e.g., Roman Catholic, Eastern or Greek Orthodox and Episcopalian) churches build their worship around centuries-old ritual that is presided over by a hierarchical priesthood. Others (particularly Baptists) are arranged into nonhierarchical communities where the focus is on Bible study and sermons offered by clergy who are called by the local community.

Still others, Quakers for example, have no presiding clergy. Rather, for Quakers, worship models Jesus' practice of prayer for guidance followed by love-based actions for peace and justice, no matter the consequences. In the silence of a simple, undecorated sanctuary, members listen first for the inner voice or, as some call it, the "Light Within." Then, when anyone speaks aloud that inner voice, others listen. Before another speaks, there is a long pause, that each person's reflections may be heard and savored.

Quaker listening extends to various discernment processes, including a "clearness committee" who "listens without prejudice or judgment" when members face particularly challenging issues. Listeners may not advise, only listen and offer "honest, probing, caring, challenging, open, loaded questions," writes Jan Hoffman in the website for the New York Yearly Meeting. "The clearness committee works best when everyone approaches it in a prayerful mood (which does not exclude playful!), affirming the reality of each person's inner guidance and truth, and the Spirit's capacity to sustain."[21]

One of the deep pains that many people at work face today is the feeling that they are neither heard, seen, or appreciated. Thus, the Quaker model for listening and discerning offers great promise for creating workplaces that are more ethical and meaningful. To adapt the Quaker model to work, however, demands that we learn to tolerate silence and the frustration of not knowing immediately what we are called to do in work or life.

Since various forms of Eastern meditation became popular in the sixties, Christians have been rediscovering their own rich mystical and contemplative traditions. Retreats at monastic abbeys offer time for reflection away from work, while monastic prayer practices are being found useful in the midst of the workday. (See the next chapter for specifics.) Copies of the prayer often credited to St. Francis, "Lord Make Me an Instrument of Thy Peace," are posted in many workstations or tucked inside desk drawers.

Human Resources consultant Roseann Roberts, in her May 2001 master's thesis for Naropa University, "Mystics in the Boardroom," considered how four spiritual teachers would encounter today's work issues. She imagines, for example, that Teresa of Avila, who had significant business experience before she co-founded the Discalced Carmelite

Order, would have particular relevance for women executives today who have lost access to their inner reserves and thus suffer a poverty of spirit.[22]

Islam: Islam (meaning "surrender") is the most recent major religion and the fastest growing. It is based on the teachings of the Koran, a sacred scripture that was received through the prayers of Mohammed beginning in the early seventh century. Islam considers the Hebrew patriarch Abraham as one of its forefathers. Its most holy place is the cube-shaped "Kaaba" in the Grand Mosque of Mecca in Saudi Arabia. According to Muslim belief, the Kaaba was raised by Abraham and his son Ishmael.

The Islamic faith is based on five pillars which must be practiced by all believers. First, there is the faith that there is only one God, Allah, and that Mohammed is his messenger. Second, there are the prayers five times daily. (For more about these and their importance, see the next chapter.) Third, there is Zakat, which includes charity and purification through giving. Fourth, there is the daily fast during the holy month of Ramadan, during which all who are physically able partake of neither food nor drink from sunup to sundown. This practice puts the focus on the spiritual world rather than the material, and increases compassionate kinship with those who go hungry due to poverty. Finally, for all who can afford it, there is Hajj, or an annual pilgrim to Mecca (or Makkah). Pilgrims cover themselves with simple robes that make it impossible to discern the wearer's class or national origin.

Islam thus requires of its adherents daily practice in the midst of daily life. Abdul Patel, a full-time systems analyst and volunteer imam (a community prayer leader) and volunteer chaplain for the University of Toronto, says that for Muslims

. . . the way of life does not separate religion or spirit from life. If you are a Muslim, you are a Muslim at the workplace,

in the street, and you carry your teachings with you everywhere. You are conscious of God's presence everywhere,
and you mold your life according to God's commands to
live a life which is beneficial to you and humanity. In the
workplace, your ethics are part of the faith as well. You
don't abuse company resources like the telephone; you
don't take stationery or supplies for home use.[23]

Islam has many other insights for work, says Iftekhar A.
Hai, Director of Interfaith Relations for the United Muslims
of America. "If every moment you know your big boss is
watching you, your behavior changes. The meaning of work
is that you have faith in God and you know that God is all
knowing, compassionate, and that he expects the highest
degree of excellence in your work."[24]

This call to excellence extends to every facet of work,
from not being involved in office politics to doing the best
work possible according to abilities. Hai continues:

> Loyalty becomes a strong contract you make not only with
> the boss, but also with your divine creator. When you put
> yourself into constant awareness of spiritual values, you
> become more compassionate, forgiving, cooperative with
> the other workers around you. You become more aware of
> the beauty within everything; you become attuned to your
> spiritual note.
>
> Of course love has to come out of that, when you are
> focused and attuned to receive love and beauty in God's
> creation. When work is done in beauty and love, you don't
> get tired, for you work in tune with a beautiful melody, the
> source of which is nothing but divine.

As a Muslim, Iftekhar Hai says he is "rent asunder" by
the stereotyping of his brethren as terrorists and/or members of radical religions. Stereotyping leads to packaged
images, which create packaged opinions, which lead to
packaged policies.

What Can You Learn from Other Faiths at Work?

Because the workplace is a primary place for meeting people of other faiths, it is also a good place for breaking stereotypes. A Christian computer executive confessed that he had denigrated Islam until several years ago when he noticed that a visiting colleague was ignoring the elegant lunch that had been laid for attendees at an important meeting. Concerned, he asked the colleague if he was well.

"This was the first time I had ever heard about Ramadan," the Christian executive said, "and I wanted to hear more. The more I heard, the more my respect grew for his religion. I can see now why this faith is spreading. It's real, because it is practiced every day."

A great way to learn about other faiths is simply to ask at lunch or during a break, "What is your basic faith and how does it relate to work?" Then listen, hopefully as respectfully and patiently as Quakers do.

Until I worked in a large law firm, I had met few Mormons. Thus, I had never learned about some practices that offer a wonderful model for integrating work life and spiritual life.

There is probably no religious group that is more committed to work-life excellence than Mormons. One night a week is family night, and even big corporate executives are known to put a family matter (e.g., attending a grandchild's ballet recital) ahead of a business meeting.

For Mormons, Jesus' commandment to "love others as you love yourself" translates into regular service to others balanced by self-care and self-responsibility. Perhaps this comes from the fact that early Mormons were pioneers who depended on each person's willingness to pull his or her weight in order for the community to survive hardships and persecution. Thus, there is an emphasis on thrift and setting aside food and funds for the inevitable time when the crops go bad or the economy turns sour.

There is also an emphasis on serving through being creative. "In my ward [the Mormon equivalent of a local parish]," a marketing specialist told me, "everyone is encouraged to develop and offer at least one creative talent, but not to build a fiefdom around that talent. Even if you're the best choir director ever, you're encouraged to stretch into other creative pursuits and allow others to learn what you've been doing. Because of this practice, I find myself willing to take more creative risks at work and support others in doing the same."

What do you think would happen if you could practice your own faith in a way that allowed you to enhance family life while doing a good job? If you combined pragmatism and creativity? If you were willing constantly to take new risks and support others as they dare to grow and stretch?

From every faith that has been mentioned, and from those that have not, there are models and insights such as these. Hopefully, you will walk away from this chapter filled with new respect for the faith of others. Hopefully, too, you will be less shy about letting the essential light of your own faith shine forth through your work, free of any dogma that would inhibit the building of a new world filled with harmony and peace.

6

Tapping Your Own Wisdom
throughout the Workday

If you have ever attended a spiritual retreat, you know how to order your day around practices that reveal the beauty and wonder of God's creation. Perhaps you also know what it is like to anchor your day in the rhythms of prayer, some of it alone and silent, some of it sung or chanted in community.

Perhaps on your retreat you found yourself speaking heartfelt thoughts before your conscious mind could censor them. Perhaps, as you washed the dishes or took out the garbage, you wondered what it would be like to work consciously every day. As you savored the richness of community during a retreat, perhaps you experienced a longing for your workplace to be less fragmented and competitive.

The more complex worklife becomes, the more we need practices that anchor us in meaning throughout the day. The faster we need to make decisions in noisy, information-overloaded settings, the more important it is to tap into our own inner stillness. And the more disconnected our work becomes from the natural rhythms of night, day, and seasons, the more we need to find our rightful place in all creation.

Two ancient models for doing all this stand out. One is Islam, the world's second largest and fastest growing faith. The other is the wisdom of centuries-old Roman Catholic religious orders. Both call us to sink into the presence of God, not just when we're stressed or in trouble, but continually throughout the day.

The Discipline of Prayer

Prayer five times a day is one of the five pillars of Islam. Prayers are required half an hour before sunrise, at midday, at midafternoon, at sunset, and before going to bed. Some prayers are done at the mosque, which builds community, but all involve kneeling and bowing, which engage the entire body in the meaning of the faith, which, in turn, can be translated as "surrender." All are done facing Mecca, the city where the holy Koran was first revealed to Mohammed. Thus, the worshiper must always orient himself or herself within the created world and faith world. "It takes a lot of discipline to maintain prayer life," says engineer Ghulam Sarwar Larik, "but the prayers give a rhythm to the day. In the morning, you pray to God as the Creator, guide, and protector. In the final prayer, which is larger, you are silent, so you can review your day and receive guidance for the next day."[1]

Business demands don't release obligations of prayer. "It's hard sometimes to obey," says Oakland business owner Chimmy Baby, "especially in winter when sunrise comes early and the workday before has been long. But you figure out what time sunrise is the next day, you set the alarm clock, and you get up and pray no matter how tired you are. If you must, you go back to bed and get more sleep, but first you pray.

"But, look, the Prophet didn't say it was going to be easy. And he understood the demands of business. His first wife was a successful businesswoman. She was the boss, and he served her, just like I have to help the boss here," he laughs, pointing to his wife Nassim. Then he says he could not imagine life without prayer. "The prayers are our strength."[2]

Prayers are also the foundation of Roman Catholic religious orders. So are other life-affirming habits. As many order members have come out of their cloisters and shed the clothing called habits, we can see more clearly some of their spiritual habits and learn from them.

The Practice of Napping

Take naps. Literally. Being connected to work twenty-four hours, seven days a week via cellphone or email is more than exhausting, demoralizing, and unhealthy; it also is inefficient. Naps, say some stress release experts, refresh the mind and body and get us going again.

Naps, say members of some religious orders, are a prime weapon against the Noonday Devil. My husband, John, who spent the first thirteen years of his adult life in the Discalced[3] Carmelites, says the term *Noonday Devil* describes the elusive sluggishness that makes one tire of being prayerful or committed. Although this can happen any time, it's more common after lunch, when energy levels tend to drop naturally.

The Noonday Devil devours good ideas and intent. Have you ever felt puzzled when one moment you feel called to do something meaningful, then suddenly it's spaceout time? When you return to the idea moments or hours or days later, does it no longer seem good? Or if it does seem like a good idea, do you wonder why bother, because who's got the energy to make the idea work?

Peptalks and self-criticism strengthen the Noonday Devil, but he evaporates in the face of practices that re-anchor you in what's meaningful and call forth the spiritual capital you need for the work to which you have been called. Sometimes that involves prayer, sometimes it calls for rolling up your sleeves and getting back to work. And sometimes it involves taking a nap or some other break that allows you to fully renew yourself.

Building a Religious Order to Life

Roman Catholic religious orders are communities of men or women who commit to a spiritual life based on a particular rule, which is similar to a constitution. The rule defines how that community lives, works, and grows spiritually. Although each order's rule is unique, it generally focuses on a simple outer life and a rich inner life where, like the Order of Carmelites, members are called to "share everything — time, incomes, wisdom, talents, and prayers. . . . Prayer is at the heart of the Carmelite rule of life, which is described as a continuous conversation with God. The Carmelite is expected to tackle the most demanding journey of all, the journey inwards into the heart."[4]

The term *religious order* can easily be turned around to *order based on religion* or *ordering life around that which holds the most meaning.* That means building order into our lives and work through spiritually based practices that create a framework for our days, much as the skeletal system creates a framework for our bodies. In creating this framework, we have much to learn from members of religious orders, no matter how different their lives may seem from ours at first glance.

Canice Johnson recently celebrated fifty years as a member of the Sisters of Mercy (RSM). At a Detroit parish celebration where she renewed her vows, she explained what her vocation means to her. "The purpose of life is to pay attention and focus on the things that bring us closer to God and other people. There are so many distractions, and many things are momentarily important. The call is to order life around the long-term things."[5]

Sister Canice and other members of religious orders exhibit two habits that those of us in the secular business world would do well to emulate. One is the habit of treating everyone as if he or she were a member of a lifelong community, even if we only meet for a moment. That means listening respectfully, thus creating a hospitable presence that incites relaxed authenticity and calls forth truthful dialogue.

Another habit is the ability to savor life fully. No one works harder than many members of religious orders; no one laughs more heartily. I recently spoke with Sister Canice, but the last time John and I saw her a few years ago, she had only a little time to spare between a workshop she was conducting and her plane back to Detroit. First, we took her to buy tap-dancing shoes. Then the three of us strolled in Golden Gate Park, where we hopped onto a calliope. There were no seats for us to sit side by side, but because Canice rode just behind me, I could hear her laughter as our painted creatures bobbed up and down. When we spoke yesterday, she laughed as we recalled that lighthearted moment. When it gets easier to cross the Canadian border again, she says she will return to the clogging group for which she bought her tap-dancing shoes.

John says that having spiritual order is like having a spiritual business plan that you regularly consult, so you can ensure that your meaningful work gets done, your meaningful life gets lived, and everything you do is done with meaning. You develop discipline, or the habit of remembering what you really want, and you act accordingly. You develop discernment, including the ability to differentiate between various psycho-physical phenomena and a grounded union with God.

Begin the Day with Commitment

One of the best places to start creating spiritual order is by consciously committing yourself to each day. My father often paused before driving to the school where he taught and we three children studied. He'd look around at the mountains that surrounded our little town of Shenandoah, Virginia, and he'd comment on something that made him happy to be alive that day. Then he'd quote, "In the morning I will set my good purpose."[6]

Biogenex CEO Krishan Kalra's workday begins with a simple prayer: "Lord, I am at your service. What is it you want me to do? Lead my day." Prayer, Kalra says, is the human version of the "home" position on a robot. "Prayer basically reconnects us with the Lord. It reorients us as to why we are here, what is our purpose, and how we should behave as human beings on a daily basis."[7]

A surprisingly popular prayer place is the shower. When a group of executives was asked where they do their most creative thinking, none said the office. Religious settings or nature tied for second place,[8] while the bathroom was number one. Einstein is reported to have gotten some of his best ideas while shaving, although for most people, the shower does it. There's something about the commitment to "come clean" physically that translates into a willingness to "come clean" mentally and spiritually. And even if we dare not sing elsewhere, making a joyful noise in the shower is acceptable in any tradition.

During one shower, the following prayer emerged. Please feel free to adapt it to your own needs.

> This is the day that God has given me,
> one day out of many before it.
> No one knows, least of all me, whether
> I shall live out this day and be granted another.
> So many days, I have been ruled by fear, pride, or self-will,
> yet even so many gifts have shown through,
> many new allies and resources developed.
> I welcome this day.
> I choose this day to dig deeper into my heart and my soul,
> to bring forth the best in me, and to bring into myself
> that which I need to be the person I was created to be.
> I do not know how this day will unfold,
> but right now I commit to its fullness,
> and I pray for the courage to live out each moment
> in wonder and love.

It doesn't take much effort to integrate prayer life with daily life. We can pray or listen to inspirational tapes while we ride the subway or practice attentiveness while we drive. We can bless our work all day and bless others as we walk past them. We can pray that each task be done for the highest good, then be willing to face our own faults and learn from them.

At lunch or other break times throughout the day, we can read devotional materials or write in a journal. We can sit alone by running water and meditate. We can do a walking meditation in which we say silently, "With each step, I recommit to hearing the voice of God in my life." We can meet with a trusted friend or spiritual director.[9]

The High Tor Alliance is a nonsectarian, nonprofit organization that supports "projects for people who are practically integrating their inner life, spirituality, and values into their workplaces and organizations."[10] Among these projects was a study on contemplative practices at work, by researchers Christopher Schaefer and Keri Darling. Respondents reported a wide variety of practices including morning meditation; using the commute time for focusing reflection and integration; doing brief centering exercises during the day; exercising attunement and reflection prior to decision making.

Respondents also offered the following comments: "Work cannot be separated from our lives and therefore becomes an integral part of our spiritual evolution." "My work is a school that teaches me about the spiritual journey." "All work is ministry in some way, if only as a place to try to model appropriate principles and values."

If you don't already know how to meditate, begin simply by sitting erect, feet flat on the floor. Breathe slowly in and out, and pay attention to what happens in your body and mind.

Perhaps you want to repeat a word or phrase from a favorite prayer to focus your attention. Thomas Keating calls this *Lectio Divina*.[11] First you read a passage from sacred Scripture and then you "rest in God" while you ponder its meaning.

Saint Ignatius of Loyola, founder of the Jesuits, developed exercises filled with questions that can readily be adapted to the workday, such as "What about my work this week (or today) has been most life-giving? What about my work has been most life-draining?" After reflecting on the answers to these questions, another prayer question is, "To what might God be calling me in these situations?"[12]

Whatever types of meditation or prayer you use, don't be hard on yourself if your mind strays. As David Roche preaches in his theatrical presentation, Church of 80% Sincerity, "Nobody can be focused and attuned all the time." So notice what itches, forgive your impure thoughts, and recommit to be still and hear the word of God.

When you order your work on your mission and purpose, menial tasks like filing take on new meaning. It's as if your mission and purpose are your heart, and each piece of paper is a capillary. When the heart of your mission is clear, you can see how it branches down from major tasks (the aorta) into sub-tasks (the various levels of arteries) and finally into the individual capillaries which feed each cell, then expel waste and send information back through a network of progressively larger veins until they meet the heart. There your blood (information system) is refreshed and revitalized before being recirculated.

In most organizations, capillary jobs such as filing and answering the telephones aren't on the organizational chart, and the people who do these jobs aren't consulted about the organization's mission or practices. When you model your filing system after your heart and circulatory system, you create a process in which you constantly discern, "Does this task/bit of information support my work or detract from it? If it is part of my work, where shall I place it so it can be found when it is needed?"

While putting away new information into old folders, it's easy to rediscover ideas and resources you've forgotten. Almost always some bits of information don't fit the system but are too intriguing to toss. Sometimes these are early messengers of a new growing edge to your work and life.

End the Day with Closure

Just as it's important to anchor a workday in meaning, it's important to relinquish the day. Carisa Bianchi, President and CEO, San Francisco Office, of the advertising agency TBWA/Chiat/Day, says:

> I worked on the Energizer Bunny campaign. And let me tell you, that little creature's very similar to advertising executives: we keep going and going. That's why I try to set an example in my office. I draw a clear line between my work life and my personal life, and I expect my co-workers to do the same. . . . When people don't take time out, they stop being productive. They stop being happy, and that affects the morale of everyone around them.[13]

In ancient times, twilight forced people to slow down and come together, perhaps to tell stories. Overhead, the night sky blazed rich in stars, even richer in the questions and mysteries it provoked. Today, however, most of us lose twilight to commute time or TV news and game shows. We believe we're too busy to sit together under the night sky and ponder the mysteries of life. If we live in cities, stars are dimmed by pollution or turned pink by crime-fighting sodium vapor light.

Unlike ancient societies whose work increased communal joy, today's workplaces often isolate workers from home and family. Thus, it becomes more important to create life-sustaining evening rituals. These rituals don't have to be complex or time-consuming. After all, it doesn't take long to read aloud with a child or to another adult; it doesn't take long to sing a hymn of thanks. Such rituals, however, make all the difference in whether or not sleep is deep and whether or not we feel ready to welcome another day.

From the interfaith community of Taize, France, come wondrous services built of simple words that are sung over and over, followed by silence, then another song and more silence. At the First Presbyterian Church in Oakland, California, services are followed by soup and salad, thereby fulfilling the words of the Taize chant, "*Ubi Caritas*," or, "Where there is caring, where there is love, there you will find God."

If you can't find a Taize service near you, it's easy to start your own.[14] Or you can simply get out some candles, play quiet music that speaks to your soul, and create your own ritual for releasing your day and preparing to welcome another.

Judging solely by the number of ads for sleeping pills, many of us have great difficulty releasing our days. Inspired by Sandy Boucher's wonderful piece on the fear of finishing (see chapter 5), here is a pre-bedtime prayer that may help welcome relaxed sleep:

> God, help me see more clearly which of my worries come from pride, self-will, or fear, and which point to genuine concerns that must be faced tomorrow. Help me turn off the chatter of ego and little mind, that I may trust the quiet, unthinking rest you now offer me. Help me remember, upon waking, the wisdom you send through my dreams, that I may be guided anew. Help me remember that all, even pain and challenge, are part of the richness that always is possible when I choose to walk not away from you, but with you.

What prayers come to you now, as you shape your own life and work around prayer itself?

7

Working with Integrity
as Your Bottom Line

During our last visit, my father and I drove up into the mountains near his home. On our way back, a sudden fog blocked all sight ahead, behind, and on either side of us. To stay safe, we had to slow down to about five miles per hour, so our headlights could identify the solid white lines that marked the right side of the twisting road.

When we were safely through the fog, Dad said, "You know, I think we're all called to be like those white lines and help guide each other through the ethical fogs of our lives."

The news today is filled with many stories of the harm that is done when people don't call one another out of ethical fogs at work. Among the headline stories of 2002 are the Enron scandal, with its huge cast of accountants and lawyers, the widespread cover-up of priestly wrongdoing, the deliberately false stock tips that were promoted by investment companies. In each of these cases, as well as lesser known examples of workplace fraud, waste, and abuse, someone went over an ethical line. Others watched them go over the line and did nothing, thus helping the fraud, waste, or abuse to continue.

Never has trust in business and nonprofit institutions been lower. Because even the most cynical people can see how the lack of trust is leading to waste of resources and even damage to the financial bottom line, no doubt there will be many more calls to redefine ethical business lines and to encourage people to police better these lines.

Important as this discussion is, it will miss the point unless it grounds the whole concept of workplace ethics in a standard deeper than the bottom line, which is *integrity*.

Integrity: The Essence of Spirit and Work

If spirit and work had to be summed up in one word, that word is *integrity*. When we live and work with integrity, we are authentic and whole. There is a beautiful resonance among body, mind, and spirit, which leads to further resonance between our values and our actions, and between ourselves and the rest of creation. Thus, when we live and work with integrity, we can express our unique viewpoint and gifts while surrendering to the call of spirit to go beyond all sense of self.

When we have integrity, we remember that we are connected to God and to a wondrous universe. To paraphrase Albert Einstein, we don't restrict ourselves to caring only for our own good or the good of a few others. Instead, we widen our "circle of compassion to embrace all living creatures and the whole of nature in its beauty."[1] Being compassionate and alert to how our actions harm or help others, we are naturally ethical. We don't lie, cheat, or steal, and we don't help others do so. Instead, we have the courage to speak out against fraud, waste, and abuse at work. We also have the courage to speak out for hope, kindness, compassion, and all the other gifts that come from being made in God's image.

When we live with integrity, we accept ourselves—faults, gifts, limitations, and all. Because we are honest with ourselves and others, we don't waste time and energy trying to keep our lies straight or worrying about living up to others' expectations. Nor do we hold back our gifts through false modesty or fear. Instead, we rest securely in the knowledge that we are loved by God in spite of our imperfections, and we give our very best to our work.

When we do our best through work, we create realistic trust, which leads to good business. "Being an ethical person is ironically a great marketing tool," says Jeff Rubin, owner of Put It in Writing newsletter service. "When you're honorable and you show people a sincere willingness to do things right, then it is easier to market and do business. It's also exciting to refer business to those who are known for giving good work, but if you just give with the expectation of getting something in return, that takes all the fun out of it."

One of Rubin's basic ethical practices is to say no to all work that does not feel right for him. Many people won't do this because they feel desperate for work, but desperation can lead to a trap in which the business and the relationships go bad. "If you don't believe that the work is out there for you, what are you doing in your business?" challenges Rubin. "Success comes when you believe in yourself and believe in the value you bring to the business world. You also have to be patient and persistent, for long-term success depends on the quality of relationships, and relationships take time."

Relationships also take trust based on clarity and accountability. Almost every weekend my nephew Chris Printz is part of an ongoing underground caving expedition that is helping to protect groundwater, bats, and other ecological treasures. After the cavers survey underground areas that have probably never before been seen by human beings, the caves are protected from further human trespass.

Some of the joy in Printz's work comes from the thrill of discovery. Equally important are the joy of service and the cooperation of people with different personalities and specialties. "Whatever is going on with us personally, we have to leave it on the surface. The only way we can work together safely is if we can count on every other member of the team to be well-trained and alert at all times," says Printz. For example, "You never know when the only way to go deeper into a cave is via passages that can only be accessed by first going up a fifty-foot wall. Though all of us have to be good at climbing, we depend on our mountain-climbing specialist to set the ropes for others to follow."

Printz finds caving deeply fulfilling. "If I am not doing this work, every ounce of my insides wants to be doing it," he says.

For artist and importer Sharon Gordon, work with integrity equals work with zest. By finding markets in the United States for artists from Zimbabwe, she helps the artists there help themselves and their communities. By selling African art in the United States, she feels as if she is honoring the spirit of her ancestors, who had been taken from their homeland long ago as slaves.

When she stood in a field in Zimbabwe in the summer of 2001 selecting sculptures, Gordon said she was "tickled from my toes to my soul." Afterwards, she worked so hard on her first show that when it was over, she sobbed with weariness, but she was happy.

"Lord, you can take me now, because this is as good as it gets," she prayed that night. Then, after a good rest, her prayer became, "Now I'm ready for the next challenge, and I can hardly wait."

Gordon recently discovered that even a summons to an IRS audit can be an integral part of meaningful work. After the IRS agent told her what information he needed, he lectured her about keeping better records. "It took me a moment or two to realize it, but that IRS agent wanted to help me succeed in business, and he was showing me how my accountant could help me do that." Immediately after the audit, Gordon integrated her filing and record-keeping practices with her spiritual practices. She then found the necessary receipt and mailed a copy to the IRS with a prayer of gratitude. "I've put too much of myself and my savings in my business to let it fail," she says. "What I do matters too much to my vendors and clients to give every aspect of it anything less than my best."

Developing the Many Facets of Integrity at Work

Wholeness. Honesty. Resonance between values and action. Zest. It takes work to create and maintain all these and other elements of integrity. Great organizations, like great lives, don't typically spring up dramatically and overnight. Instead, they are based on a formula as simple as the combination of Shakespeare's admonition, "To thine own self be true" and Mother Teresa's admonition to do small deeds with great love.

Like all simple formulas, this one can be very difficult to follow, for human beings are complex and often contradictory creatures. As much as we want to see our way clear to a life based on integrity, we also fog our sight and fight the callings of our own hearts.

As I learned by studying a personal memory from when I was in the fifth grade, it's possible to lose integrity very quickly. When a classmate gave me poetry he had written and jewelry he had bought by saving his allowance for several months, I was thrilled. Then a girlfriend read the poem over my shoulder and teased, "Oooh, you don't like him, do you?" I looked at him, standing on the other side of the playground watching for my reaction. I then looked back at my friend, a few inches away, her face filled with disgust. "No, I don't like him," I lied, immediately regretting my words.

Every day in workplaces, supposed adults act no better, for the workplace is filled with former fifth graders who learned that it isn't cool to be more obedient to our core values than to the fads and mores of the predominant culture. The deeper truth is that underneath our most terrible faults are gifts that shine forth our likeness to God. Seeing these gifts in ourselves and others is truly awesome. Helping each other bring forth these gifts, in spite of our fears, is even more awesome.

From the ancient Hebrew prophets—Jonah, Isaiah, Ezekiel, Nathan—we can learn much about the longing for and fear of knowing and speaking truth. Being prophets is never easy, for who among us really means, "Thank you for sharing that," when someone calls us to face a fault or illusion. Who among us does not fear that, if we believe the really good news, we will be disappointed.

When we are prophets to one another at work, we become leaders—like Jesus, who can see our worst faults, such as Peter's betrayal of him three times in one night—yet still entrust one another with valuable work. As we help one another see our gifts, we can build solid businesses and service organizations based on our deepest values.

Just as every religion has rules, such as the Ten Commandments, to help the faithful know whether they are in or out of harmony with God, every profession has its rules and practices for determining whether or not work has integrity. Accounting, for example, has its practices for discerning whether money is handled ethically and in a way that results in profit, not loss. Health and legal professions also have their standards for ethical and effective conduct. Building trades have a whole array of codes, standards, and instruments for determining whether something is built "on true."

For thousands of years, builders have known how to build "on true" by using the plumb (a weight on a string) to measure vertical alignment and the level (a small clear container almost filled with liquid that is encased in a flat piece of wood) to measure horizontal alignment. These ancient tools can also be used as symbols to guide a meditation to discover whether or not you are "on true."[2]

Imagine the plumb as an invisible line for aligning all the parts of yourself (intuition, legs, heart, brain, etc.) so each can do its proper work. Imagine that the plumb line extends down into the core of the earth, helping you attune to current reality with all its hopes and challenges. Finally, imagine that the line extends all the way through the earth and then throughout the whole cosmos, guiding you to alignment with the source of ultimate reality.

Here, in this place of alignment of self to self, of self to ultimate reality, sight is clearer. A friend says, "When I'm off true, I can deny a problem and obsess over it at the same time. I can paralyze myself and wear myself out with frenetic behavior. When I'm 'on true,' I can face the challenge and deal with it gracefully."

An almost full plastic water bottle makes an excellent level. When the air bubble inside the bottle is perfectly centered, the bottle is level. Tipped one way, the level reminds one worker how easy it is to get self-absorbed and selfish. Tipped another way, it reminds her of the opposite tendencies to become enmeshed in others' lives. When she's on true, she can see clearly how her compassion works well with her need for healthy boundaries. Thus, she can be engaged with others without being swallowed up by them. She can serve others without diminishing their own capacity to grow.

Whatever external rules and standards we use, they need to be balanced with diligent action and compassionate wisdom. Fortunately, all of us are endowed by our Creator with many gifts that help us discern whether we are walking toward or away from a path of integrity.

Those gifts begin with basic instincts. Perhaps you can recall biology classes in which you watched amoebas move naturally toward that which was good for them and away from that which was not. Or perhaps you've experienced a physical feeling of revulsion when you were doing something you knew to be wrong or saw someone else act without integrity. Does your chest expand and joy ripple throughout your body when you know you are doing something you are called to do or you are inspired by the good deeds of others? Can you feel the difference between puffed-up pride and true self-respect?

"We all have unique integrity signals," says Ron Bedrick, an attorney and business consultant, "but it takes practice to become sensitive to the specific feelings and sensations that let us know when we, the heart is the point of reference, for the heart is the source of inner wisdom which allows me to decide how to act in any situation."

Bedrick is intrigued by gyroscopes, which remain on course regardless of the external forces that impinge upon them.

> Gyroscopes are incorporated in navigation equipment to help it achieve the purpose for which it was created. Just as the gyroscope plays the key role in maintaining original motion, the heart plays a key role for balancing us between opposites and keeping us on course. We can use the power of the heart to neutralize potentially distorting emotions, so we can choose to embody and express our highest potentials.[3]

My father taught me to see that integrity, like love, is a moment-to-moment choice. Will I exercise my integrity muscles, or will I let them atrophy from nonuse? Will I starve those muscles, poison them with cynicism or justifications, or feed them inspiring thoughts and practical stories?

Being White Lines of Integrity for One Another

At the height of the Great Depression, when Dad was in his twenties, he faced unemployment unless he accepted a new job based on a fraud. Momentarily, while standing on the remains of an old bridge he was helping to demolish, Dad felt tempted by the fear of what might happen if he followed his conscience, and by the image of what he might win if he ignored his conscience. Then a Canadian goose flew close by and eyeballed him. It seemed to say, "You know you've got to do the right thing."

For the first time in his career, Dad lost his footing. As he scrambled for balance, he remembered Psalm 121, which promises that he would be guarded from evil, "both now and forever."

After regaining his footing, Dad formally refused the new job and soon found fulfilling new work that allowed him to complete college and graduate school. This led to an offer to create an industrial arts department at a college in another state. There he met my mother, and there he found a wonderful camaraderie among other teachers and staff.

Six months after I was born, Dad discovered that he had unwittingly helped his boss, the college president, embezzle. Receipts Dad had approved for paying casual labor had been altered by the president, who then pocketed the tenfold difference. A load of cement, which Dad had accepted on the president's behalf for personal real estate projects, was actually paid for with a state check.

On the advice of a state senator, Dad met with the state bureau of investigation, who used his information to conduct a supposedly routine audit. Then Dad resigned and we moved out of state because Dad was warned, "The president can get you in jail for slander easier than we can indict him for embezzlement."

Although Dad was an anonymous whistleblower, he was slandered, and he suffered emotionally as the investigation and trial dragged on four years. Worse, he watched his former colleagues and students suffer as the powerful president slandered, even fired, those who did not support him. Dad's best friend on the faculty died not long after from a heart attack; another had a stroke.

Dad later realized that the president's embezzling was supported by a complex system of ingrained beliefs, including, "If you can't say something good about anyone, don't say anything at all." Other rules and mores held that it is bad to question authority or to expose a group to public scrutiny. There's a seemingly universal fear that the words "I don't trust this about you" are necessarily hurtful, not an invitation to respectful dialogue. And then there are all those taboos against "tattling," which we learned at home and on the playground.

It takes a lot of courage and work to fight a lack of integrity in self and others. It takes even more work, however, to maintain a lack of integrity. That's the theme of the popular children's fable, "The Emperor's New Clothes," in which an empire's bottom line was enhancing the emperor's vanity, particularly his passion for parading hourly in new clothes.[4] How the populace felt about this great waste of resources and lack of leadership is unknown, for people throughout the empire were afraid to do anything that would make the emperor feel bad about himself. They also hoped that, by enhancing the emperor's vanity, they would win.

By surrounding himself with people who dared not speak the truth, the emperor set himself up for betrayal by those he trusted. No one, not even the prime minister, who was known for good sense, dared admit he could not see what two scoundrels claimed was cloth "so light and fine that it looks invisible . . . to anyone who is too stupid or incompetent to appreciate its quality." Nor did the emperor dare admit he saw nothing, and so he eventually paraded naked in front of the cheering populace, until a small child dared speak the truth, and the populace gained the courage to chant out the child's truth.

Even so, the father of that child tried to shush the boy. Meanwhile, the emperor denied the truth and the procession continued, with the emperor's page continuing to hold his arms aloft as if they contained a real train, and not a figment of the emperor's illusion.

Some popular versions of the story today have rewritten Hans Christian Andersen's ending to make the emperor reward the child for telling the truth. Andersen's original ending, however, is much closer to everyday reality.

In late January 2002, *Workforce* magazine, which caters to human resources executives and managers, conducted an on-line poll. By January 22, 567 people had responded. Only 39 percent thought that if they warned their CEO of a potential crisis, he or she would listen; 31 percent did not expect the CEO to listen. In response to another question, only 51 percent of the respondents said their corporate culture was "such that an employee can approach the CEO on a controversial matter." Thirty-three percent said their corporate culture did not support such an approach.[5] If a similar survey were taken of rank-and-file employees in businesses, nonprofit organizations, and religious institutions, the percentage of people who feel free to speak up or expect to be heard would probably be much lower.

Since ancient tribal times, humans have always depended on the integrity of others. When that integrity has been missing, we all suffer.

At work, we have an enormous capacity to harm others. When we fail to speak our doubts about suspicious invoices, we help create a climate where fraud can thrive. When we help a drug company repress information about the side effects of one of its products or a manufacturer to repress information about the pollution it creates, we contribute to the illness or deaths of people we may never meet.

The more complex our society becomes, the more capacity we have to harm others we may never know. Thus, more than ever we need courageous whistleblowers to protect us from workplace fraud, waste, and abuse, just as we need police or soldiers to protect us from crime or invading warriors.

Yet, although we are told from childhood that we are supposed to tell the truth, we are rarely told how to do it effectively. Few of us know how to confront others effectively and compassionately. We don't get much support from our faith communities about how to act for the good without martyring ourselves in the process. We don't get many stories and examples about what a gift it could be to say to another, "I think you're out of line" and to be willing to listen when another thinks we're out of line.

"If someone had long ago told my old boss, 'No, Dr. Meadows, you can't take so much as one penny from the college,' that person would have done the boss a great favor," Dad once said. If he had been confronted early by caring people, the boss might have ended his days surrounded by family and friends, not prison bars.

As we talk about the prevention of future Enrons or church scandals or all the other ethical fogs, perhaps it's time to re-read the fable of the emperor and his new clothes. Some questions it suggests for individuals and groups are:

- How much do you structure your life and work around your pride, fear, or self-will rather than your core values?
- How willing are you to see or speak about a flaw in a product or service when others are excited about potential profits or other benefits?
- How do you help implement policies you believe to be wasteful, fraudulent, or abusive?
- How scared are you, like the father of the child in "The Emperor's New Clothes," that your "childish" gifts such as intuition or honesty will get you in trouble?
- What does it cost to deny lapses of integrity — your own or that of others?
- How can you help restore and maintain integrity in your organization?

Making Integrity Our Bottom Line

From the legal profession at its best come two models for building our work and organizations on a bottom line of integrity. One is the system of contracts, or formal agreements based on clarity, not assumptions. Stewart Levine, author of *Getting to Resolution: Turning Conflict into Collaboration* and the forthcoming *Book of Agreements*,[6] sees the potential for agreements to "build partnerships based on deep covenant."

In the poem "Agreements," Levine says that agreements "guide us, and ground us, and focus collaboration. . . . They articulate joint vision, and set a clear plan. They build deeper trust. . . . With the great gifts of agreements in place, it's easier by far, to reach states of grace."

A second legal model is a system of justice making. Although the legal system is often characterized as only adversarial, recent transformative movements have included collaborative law (especially among divorce attorneys who agree to work with their clients to settle their issues outside court) and restorative justice, which seeks to heal victims, wrongdoers, and the society at large.

A great story about restorative justice and reclaiming integrity is Charles Dickens's *A Christmas Carol*, in which the miserly and embittered Ebenezer Scrooge is met by the ghost of his equally miserly and embittered partner, Jacob Marley. Thus begins a spiritual journey into the past, present, and future that turns Scrooge, overnight, into a man whose generosity encompasses the sharing of his wealth, time, and love.

Note that the guiding spirits don't just show Scrooge where he is out of integrity and the consequences of his choices. They also show him what it once meant for him to receive and give love, to live and work with meaning and joy. They help him see how his refusal to grieve or forgive led to the choice to withhold his gifts from others and from himself. Then, through new cracks in the armor around his heart, compassion grows and a new vision for work and life takes root.

The essential premise of *A Christmas Carol* inspires great questions for people of any faith:

- Who is your equivalent of Jacob Marley, the messenger who knows you so well that you cannot ignore him or her? What does your messenger say?
- What scenes from your past help you remember what it's like to live or work with integrity? What scenes help you learn more about your choices to move out of integrity?
- What current consequences do you see from past choices and current actions? What steps could you take to

reclaim your integrity and build upon a firmer foundation? What support and blessings are available for you?

8

Creating Spiritual Community
at and for Your Work

Every Christmas, the movie *It's a Wonderful Life* replays its themes of meaningful work amidst meaningful community. Granted, the movie is simplistic, for rarely are work issues resolved so quickly and dramatically as when George Bailey chooses to appreciate his life and work. And none of us is so important or surrounded by so many spineless people who lack courage that without us, our whole town would fall apart.

Yet, George Bailey personifies themes that even cynics can appreciate. Who doesn't yearn sometimes to trade the daily grind for daily adventure. Whose livelihood doesn't feel threatened by the carelessness of people like Uncle Billy.

In the fictional Bedford Falls, we see people celebrate one another's successes and pitch in for one another when the going gets rough. In one scene, George and Mary Bailey have helped a family move into their first decent home after George helped create the community's first affordable housing. Mary offers three symbolic gifts: bread (that this house may never know hunger); salt (that life may always have flavor); and wine (that joy and prosperity may reign forever).[1]

Many new spiritual journeys will probably rise from this moment. Here, where love dwells, children can grow up to give back more gifts to the community and the world at large. Undoubtedly, there will be many more examples like this of everyday communion.

Building Spiritual Community

Communion in the midst of community. Isn't that we all really want?

That's another gift we can learn to model from religious orders. As David Snowdon writes in *Aging with Grace*, nuns live much longer and healthier lives than the average woman. In a study he has conducted since 1986 with members of the School Sisters of Notre Dame,[2] he wrote that faith and community are a major reason for the sisters' unusual longevity and vitality. "Profound faith, like a positive outlook, buffers the sorrows and tragedies that all of us experience. . . . The community not only stimulates their minds, celebrates their accomplishments, and shares their aspirations, but also . . . understands their defeats, and nurtures them when their bodies fail them."

That's the kind of community that my friend Sister Canice Johnson has enjoyed for fifty years. Sister Canice doesn't know how different her life would be had she not become a Sister of Mercy, but she notes,

> I can't imagine a life without having walked with these wonderful women over the years. Often we had conversations over supper or over morning prayer that stretched me in ways I wasn't ready for, whether politically or spiritually or theologically. But I grew ready.
>
> Religious orders don't have a corner on spiritual community, but our lifestyle leads us to understand how important it is to walk our way with other people. Anybody needs to find other people who have an interest in spirituality and in their own development, and they need to invite those other people to challenge them.

Building spiritual community in secular workplaces requires creativity, not only because workers come from diverse faiths, but because laws prohibit overtly religious language or rituals. Yet, the secular meaning of the word communion—sharing common thoughts and participating in activities that build strong bonds—can be facilitated anywhere. My sister, Peggy Printz, a conservative Christian who loves being a mental health case manger in rural Virginia, is excited by the team-building rituals conducted by her Jewish supervisor, Nansy Steinhorn.

Steinhorn recently facilitated a reflection about the group's mission and purpose. After passing around a dish of kosher salt, she invited employees to share whatever came to them about the properties of salt and how their work in some way resembles salt. Here are some responses:

- Salt was one of the first preservatives. We help clients regain what they lost during years of mental illness, such as relationships or places in society. We also help them preserve whatever gains they make as a result of working with us.
- Salt makes people thirsty. We help clients thirst for more knowledge, more skills, more connectedness, more hope, and a greater sense of possibility.
- Salt is a catalyst for change, as in creating new colors of dyes that can be painted on silk. We are catalysts for our clients, helping them find new colors and textures within themselves.
- Salt is an important element in blood. We need to remember how important we are to our clients' lives.
- Salt is mentioned in the Russian proverb, "Eat bread and salt and tell the truth." Our work is to tell the truth and help provide the basics that our clients need, even when we're challenged by HMO or Medicare regulations.

This exercise contributed to community spirit because no participation was forced. Any reaction was welcome, which is particularly necessary when groups are not used to doing creative, off-the-wall exercises.

Peggy, who has worked at the center for fourteen years, says,

> You can tell we have a healthy workplace, because we know immediately if someone is having a bad day. A lot of burden-lifting happens spontaneously. We can deal with misunderstandings because we're free to disagree and be different, and we know that our unique contributions will be acknowledged and appreciated instead of just tolerated.
>
> When we support each other through personal challenges at work, we create bonds that make us stronger people. This isn't stealing time and energy from work, but helping us deal with things more quickly and easily because we don't have to waste energy pretending to be someone we're not or figuring out what someone else really means.

Communion in the Secular Sphere

The hunger for community like this is a main motivator of the spirit and work movement. It begins with individuals who speak their joys and concerns about work and who listen to the joys and concerns of others. Out of this heartfelt sharing, community grows. It may not be as committed and close-knit a community as that in religious orders, but it is the kind of community that works well in secular lives.

In late 1994, Episcopal divinity student Whitney Roberson joined church-sponsored focus groups with downtown San Francisco business people about how the Church could best support their spiritual and professional lives. "We'd been sitting around the table for almost an hour," writes Roberson in *Spirituality at Work: A Handbook for Conversation Convenors and Facilitators*,[3] "sorting through our frustrations about work: a disappointing lack of trust, uncertain job security coupled with an increasing workload, the longing for greater connection and meaning. 'What are the questions which come out of our stories?' the conversation facilitator had just [asked]. The business professionals fell silent for a moment, reflecting soberly. Then an attorney spoke into the silence, 'My question is simple, really: Wherein lies our hope?'"

This question inspired Roberson to focus her theological studies on spirituality and work. She envisioned conversations that facilitate communities of encouragement and empowered members to integrate fully faith and work. After graduation and ordination, Roberson published the *Handbook*, which contains "agendas" for conversations filled with compelling questions and quotes from many traditions.

In a typical conversation, participants connect through a question such as, "What work-related concern is most on your mind at the moment?" Next follows a reading from scriptures, from a story, or from a book followed by silent reflection, then more questions. For example, here are three from anthropologist Angeles Arrien in one agenda: "What surprised me today? What moved me today? What inspired me today?"

The agenda suggests allowing more time to reflect, record notes, and share insights, followed by suggestions for applying the wisdom of the hour to the workday. In closing, each person turns to the person on the left and offers a sentence of hope or blessing for the coming week. This simple ritual always seems to evoke just the right blessing, even if, only an hour before, participants had not yet met.

Elizabeth Doty, CEO and Creative Director of Bridge Interactive (a specialized interactive media company that supports learning in business), helps people find meaning by building authentic community. Doty is the founder of the nonprofit Business Storytellers, whose members use simple guidelines to create the essence of a campfire under a starry sky during meetings in office conference rooms or public meeting rooms.[4]

"We have discovered," she says, "that work experiences profoundly affect how we make meaning of life. Business Storytellers gives us a place to be seen and heard, then follow stories into learning, solutions, and action."

Doty notes that there are two main ways that people find meaning through work:

One is giving your gifts to the world through work that comes from some source in you, the kind of work that suits your talents and passions. There is also the process of finding meaning in any work by how you go about the practice of working. The latter idea excites me, because imagine how healthy our society would be if people did all work with a sense of meaning.

I'm worried that too many people see meaning only in the first definition. When people think they have to leave the corporate world to find meaning, the corporation becomes hollow. We need people at all levels of the corporation who care deeply about what they do. Otherwise, we're all impoverished.[5]

One reason storytelling is so important is that the stories we tell each other at work are far more likely to promote negative beliefs about meaningful work than positive beliefs.

Many negative workplace stories carry two distinct themes: 1) work necessarily is exhausting and demeaning; and/or 2) there's something wrong with us if we can't take the pressure that everyone else presumably can handle so well. "People assume their workplace has a 'norm' when it really doesn't," says Christina Paslach, professor of psychology at the University of California in Berkeley, "so a company wide ignorance develops. Since people don't talk about how they're struggling, everyone thinks that everyone else is handling things fine. Companies with employee burnout have major communication work to do."[6]

Negative workplace stories are like junk food. They may quash awareness of spiritual hunger pains, but they are never fully satisfying. They may carry tips for how to be a little more balanced or comfortable with our lives, but they don't help us ask the questions that could create work-life excellence.

By contrast, the stories that emerge from a typical Business Storytellers group or the type of conversations that Roberson suggests spread hope. Participants go beyond complaining about work problems, to speak their pain and generate creativity that lets them see new options. They create spiritual ties that allow individual insights to flow into the greater wisdom of the community and back again.

People in business want to speak about spirit, says Sarah Hargrave, a Science of Mind minister and owner of Hargrave Consulting. She has conducted monthly spirituality-and-work breakfast conversations for more than ten years. She was inspired to do this after serving as corporate director of marketing and public affairs for Sears Roebuck & Co. and as Vice President and Treasurer of the Sears-Roebuck Foundation.

Hargrave loved this work and felt truly called to it, but she felt split between its demands and the spiritual studies that filled her weekends and evenings. Friends and colleagues said they also wanted to bring their business worlds and their spiritual lives together, but they didn't know how to do so within their busy professional lives.

After moving to California and starting her own business, Hargrave eventually created three breakfast meeting groups for which the theme or topic is announced prior to each gathering. She begins by speaking about the topic for a maximum of five minutes, then she offers a question for reflection. Discussion follows, and the group ends with specific intentions for bringing more spirit into their work.

About five years ago, Hargrave spoke at a Business Women's Roundtable at the San Francisco Chamber of Commerce to a standing-room-only crowd. With Debra Mugnani Monroe, president of Monroe Personnel Services LLC/Temp Time in San Francisco, Hargrave then created a flexible format for monthly ongoing conversations at the Chamber of Commerce that have continued for more than four years.

After a candle-lighting ritual and a brief silence, a participant randomly selects an initial topic question from previous group suggestions. To encourage careful listening and a comfortable pace, a "talking stick" is used. One person takes it, speaks, then returns the stick to the table. After a pause, another person takes the stick and speaks.

"There are very few places in the financial district where people can gather and feel comfortable talking about spirit," says Monroe. "Here, people connect with other business people who also search for what Steven Covey calls 'due north,' or the point of deepest truth and meaning. There's a lot of love here, and people typically leave with a feeling that their loads are lighter."[7]

Monroe says that sometimes she gets so busy at work that she wonders how she can possibly help facilitate a conversation about spirit and work. "By forcing myself to pause and remember what really matters, and by connecting with others, I reconnect to my own spiritual practices. During meetings, people almost always experience shifts in their thinking. Sometimes they see different ways of approaching what seemed an insurmountable problem; sometimes they realize something really isn't such an important problem after all."

Monroe says the conversations are not networking events, but community building. "Many people come regularly. They choose to stay in touch between meetings through email or in person."

Another type of community forms when people come together for conferences or discussions about particular topics. An example of the latter is the Presidio Dialogues[8] which were started by futurist and author John Renesch. Here members of the community have a unique opportunity to hear brief, pro bono presentations from well-recognized experts on specific topics. "The presenters put the bones together upon which dialogue happens. Then we open the dialogue to everyone," says Renesch.

Great care is taken to ensure that the events are true to their purpose, which is not professional networking but the creation of a public venue where people feel safe to talk openly about "matters that matter. For a public meeting, people feel remarkably safe to share private thoughts."

Initially, Renesch thought that the specific question posed for each evening's dialogue would be the major draw. Instead, it has been the presenters themselves who draw the audience. They then draw the group into the discussion of the topic.

The Presidio Dialogues are intended not to stand alone. Thus, Renesch hopes that the work they have done to create dialogues in San Francisco will be a template that people in other areas can use to create their own dialogues. He also has plans for recording the Dialogues and placing them on the website, so people anywhere can watch a meeting and participate through online dialogue.

The Presidio Dialogues owe much of their success to the fact that John Renesch has spent many years building relationships among people who are committed to various aspects of spirit and work. They also build on the power of the ripple effect, for whatever good is done by one, its ripples spread out and touch others.

Thus, individuals everywhere can help create community simply by letting their spirits ripple out into their workplace. As one receptionist, now known as a powerful spirit-lifter, discovered, one person's ripples can profoundly impact the spirit and energy of those around her.

This receptionist became severely depressed after she was transferred from working among people she loved to a new situation among comparative strangers. At the time, the firm was undergoing tumultuous changes. Staff had been laid off and much of the firm's space had been re-let. Many people who were used to private offices were being pushed into small cubicles that offered no privacy. Everyone was being shuffled as remaining space was redesigned.

"The new space felt like a confused rabbit warren at first," the receptionist said. "Though all of us shared common feelings of loss and despair, we just couldn't seem to connect. When they passed my desk, staff mostly ignored me or spread a little anger and fear every time they passed."

Each day, for more than a month, the receptionist vented her frustrations with her husband after work. Finally, her husband refused to hear anymore complaints. "Either find a way to make this job work better for you," he said, "or get another job."

That night the receptionist prayed hard. "That was a turning point," she said. "I realized that instead of dealing with how lost I felt when I was reassigned — the loss of continuity, security, comfortable patterns, as well as colleagues — I got stuck feeling sorry for myself. Though I was surrounded by many more people than before, I felt isolated because I hadn't given people a chance."

The woman vowed then to be kind and cheerful to everyone she met the next day, no matter how she felt. "I thought, can I perhaps enhance their day by acknowledging them individually by something so simple as a smile?"

At first, she had to force her smiles a bit. But her compassion for co-workers soon grew, which took away her grief and discomfort. It became natural to give out smiles and words that conveyed genuine blessing and an acknowledgement of each person's worth.

The woman's sense of humor also returned and was multiplied by staff who took her good wishes to their cubicles, where they spread a bit of their own. Then, as blessing multiplied on blessing, stress levels dropped and cooperation and morale soared. "I'm still stunned," the receptionist recently told me, "by how positive the repercussions were from the simple choice to smile and acknowledge everyone. Smile by smile, we made a difference for each other."

Serving together is a great way to build workplace spirit. Community organizations like Christmas in April can always use help. It's amazing how much you can learn about a co-worker or boss when you paint a house or pull weeds together!

Members of a small San Francisco law firm have enjoyed creative ways to give to a charity they select together. For several months each year, staff members donate baked goods, and nibblers "pay" for these treats with contributions to the charity. One year, staff members held a silent auction, where they bought one another's plants, toys, videos, artwork, and other items and donated the proceeds. Shortly before Christmas, the firm matched the amount that had been raised through employee activities, and everyone shared the joy of what they had done together.

That firm also honored the passing of a staff member who was estranged from his family. After deciding that they were all the family he had, all who wished to do so gathered in a tulip garden at Golden Gate Park. An altar was built with a small table, cloth, and objects that held meaning to the deceased and his relationships in the firm. Each attendee said aloud prayers and blessings from any tradition. After the service, the firm invited everyone to lunch, where the bonding of the living continued.

Creating Your Own Sense of Community

What kind of spiritual community do you now enjoy in your own place of business? What stories in this chapter inspire you to create something new?

Here are some further ideas and guidelines for building spiritual community at work.

Don't let workplace camaraderie replace community in the rest of your life. Remember that you have many communities: family, friends, professional organizations, creative groups, service projects, your neighborhood, your faith community. It's tempting to use one type of community to avoid dealing with others. Many people (recall the boss who bragged he was so loyal to his firm that he missed the births of all four of his children) use the busyness of business to avoid developing intimate family or social relationships. Many firms offer services to encourage employees to stay at work longer.

If you spend too much time at work, it's easy to become so estranged from other relationships that you are tempted

to spend even more time at work. This saps your creative
energy and all your spirit. If you lose your job, you could feel
utterly lost.

Aim for balance so that each of your communities supports the other. Let healthy relationships at home help create
healthy relationships at work, which, in turn, help create
healthy relationships in faith communities and vice versa.

Look for opportunities to open dialogue about spirit and work. The
overwhelming majority of people are interested in spirit and
work, but they may feel just as shy as you do talking about
it. Here are some ways to encourage dialogue:

- List your most compelling questions about spirit and
  work and, on break, ask trusted colleagues if they
  have similar questions.
- At a networking meeting, ask if others would like to
  discuss points raised by a book you found meaningful. (Often people feel freer to speak about meaningful
  issues through the vehicle of a book discussion.)
- Present a paper or speak at a networking group or
  conference that relates research and your own experiences of meaningful work to your field.
- Write an article about spirit and work for your organization's local and/or national newsletters, or
  encourage one of your group's good writers to do so.
- Let meeting planners and newsletter editors know of
  your interest. Suggest specific topics and speakers or
  authors whose views you'd appreciate hearing dis-
  cussed.
- Create a special interest group (SIG). Organizational
  development consultant Diane Fleck calls the Consciousness in Action SIG that she created for the
  American Society of Training and Development "a
  practical forum for how others are bringing a sense of
  meaning, purpose, and spirit to their work." Monthly
  meetings regularly draw fifteen to thirty participants

who share insights and inspiration for professional development, mentoring, fun, and creativity.[9]

Utilize technology to support community. Whitney Roberson and Mary Wagner, Director of the Center for Education and Human Services Research at Stanford Research Institute (SRI), facilitate an online course that draws people from several countries. Each participant posts a homepage that allows others to "meet" him or her. Every day or two, a new reflection question or exercise is posted. As participants respond, they read others' insights. An online course for facilitators is planned, as are projects for young adults.

Elizabeth Doty is excited that a group in Switzerland used information from the Business Storytellers website to develop groups in their country. That inspired Doty to post storytelling topics and questions from the business storytelling groups of which she is a part. The joy of sharing ideas freely, says Doty, is that, "you never know where they will take root or how far they will go."

Never push your beliefs or spiritual practices on others. For Mary Wagner, the most important guideline in talking about spirit at work is hospitable common sense. "What works for me is to stay as truly and honestly in touch with my own faith as I can. Everything grows out of that. If your faith is different and I am centered in mine, I will treat you as someone sacred and divine. If you can reach other people from that place, then hospitality naturally flows. Respect naturally flows."

9

Envisioning and Re-Visioning
Your Work and Your Profession

How can we create a culture that has more moral energy and depth?

All through the early months of 1915, Dr. Albert Schweitzer pondered that question as he went about his work of tending the sick in the medical clinic he had founded in Lambarene, West Africa. The question was not just a personal fascination, for Schweitzer's publishers were eager to publish a book on the subject, and new book royalties were always needed to support the clinic. Writing time was scarce, however, for much of Schweitzer's limited "free time" had to be spent practicing Bach cantatas so he could keep up the musical skills that also helped finance the hospital.

Thus, Schweitzer determined to make the most of a slow steamboat journey to tend the wife of a Swiss medical missionary some 120 miles upriver. Despite Schweitzer's experience as an author and his well-developed scholarly discipline, however, his persistence yielded only pages of disconnected sentences. It was as if the answer to his problem lay behind a dense thicket, which itself was behind a locked iron door.

At sunset on the third day of the journey, the boat stopped near the village of Igendja. Schweitzer looked up to see why. He later wrote:

> On a sandbank to our left, four hippopotami and their young plodded along in our direction. Just then, in my great tiredness and discouragement, there flashed upon my mind, unforeseen and unsought, the phrase, "Reverence for Life."

The iron door had yielded: the path in the thicket had become visible. Now I had found my way to the idea in which affirmation of the world and ethics are contained side by side! As far as I knew, it was a phrase I had never heard nor ever read. I realized at once that it carried within itself the solution to the problem that had been torturing me. Only by means of reverence for life can we establish a spiritual and human relationship with both people and all living creatures within our reach.[1]

Schweitzer's examples of reverence for life inspired numerous acts of creative service. At least four hospitals were named after him, one by Larry Mellon, who used his inheritance from a steel fortune to become a doctor and build a hospital in Haiti. Hugh O'Brien, star of the fifties TV show, *Wyatt Earp*, was inspired by his visit with Schweitzer to found a youth organization that is still active. Artist-dentist-writer Frederick Franck returned from service with Schweitzer to write his groundbreaking work, *The Zen of Seeing: Seeing and Drawing as Meditation.*[2]

Rachel Carson dedicated her groundbreaking book *Silent Spring* to Schweitzer. She, like Schwietzer, is frequently honored as a visionary, for she helped us see, long before the space program returned the first views of our fragile planet suspended in space, that all who dwell on earth are interconnected. Now, inspired by *Silent Spring* and the environmental movement it launched, the overwhelming majority of people throughout the world have recognized that we simply must be more conscious of the impact of technology and human attitudes on the rest of creation. Many of us are also discovering that, like Schweitzer, we can find powerful guidance for our lives by getting out into the world and letting it teach us.

Discovering the Power of Vision

Although few people are recognized as visionary, the ability to be visionary is not rare. All of us are endowed with many potentials that together create vision. Among these are imagination, intuition, hope, curiosity, physical senses, playfulness, memory, and logic. Accompanying these potentials are various catalytic attitudes including the willingness not to know an answer, an ability to consider seemingly contradictory information, an open mind and heart, humility, self respect, and creative courage.

Simply by holding a vision and daring to want its fulfillment, we call forth what is needed to turn vision into reality: creativity, resourcefulness, courage, and the motivation to keep going through hard times. Our enthusiasm for building a vision naturally draws allies who share a dream and can help turn it into reality.

Like a "Search" function on a computer, visions give us the ability to quickly weed through information overload and find what's most relevant, what's attuned to our integrity, and what is not. By following a vision, we stretch our talents and learn more about ourselves. Thus, following a vision will always be satisfying, even if the end result is very different from what we originally imagined.

Where integrity meets creativity, vision naturally grows. On this fertile ground of our most powerful potential, we can see clearly a path to meaningful and joyful work. Individually, we become more focused and resourceful. We can see more clearly the work to which we are called, whether that means a call to a specific vocation or a call to find new meaning and joy in any job.

When we are the visionaries we were born to be, we see more clearly the gifts and faults in our field of work. Like Patsy Attwood (see chapter 3) and the transferred receptionist (see chapter 8), we see the potential for ministry and personal growth in frustrating or supposedly mundane work.

Like Steve Keeva and Carole Peccorini (see chapter 2), we see ways to liberate the heart and soul in our professions. Like Whitney Roberson and Elizabeth Doty (see chapter 8), we see how to encourage meaningful connection, that we might bring more caring and health to the healthcare field, more accountability to the accounting profession, more service to the field of customer service.

Like new love, vision can appear suddenly. One moment we are alone or without direction, the next moment we have found a potential new love or direction. More often, vision, like love, grows slowly as new dimensions are seen in the familiar, or new hope emerges from old problems.

One way to invite new visions for work and life is to simply notice the stories in this book or elsewhere that inspire you and ask, "How might this apply to my situation? What new ideas does this story inspire?"

Spirit and work discussion groups are wonderful places to invite visions. For group visioning as well as individual visioning, experiment with a variety of methods. Share ideas and inspirational stories. Experiment with your imagination. Pray and be silent.

Questing for a Vision

Some questions, like "What am I called to do with my life?" or "How are we called to make our profession more ethical?" or "How can we create a culture that has more moral energy and depth?" call for the extended prayer and patience of a vision quest.

In ancient societies, questing for a vision was a ritualized part of growing up. That quest involved a long period of training followed by a period of prayer in isolation from the community, during which youth found their spirit guides and their place within the created world.

Today, many people find that elements of a traditional vision quest are important elements of the spiritual life. For example, spending a few days alone in the wilderness in prayer and modified fasting will almost surely open the doors to new perceptions and insights for work and life.

Most of us, however, must do our vision-questing in the midst of daily life. Fortunately, everyday vision-questing, particularly if it is practiced throughout life, can be a powerful and authentic spiritual practice. The one who inspired the term, "everyday vision-questing," is Albert Schweitzer.

As a young man, Schweitzer vowed that by the time he was thirty, he would devote his life to service. Until he knew the nature of that service, he decided to follow whatever professions fascinated him.

Soon, Schweitzer developed mastery as a theologian, a professor, a writer, and a master organist and builder of organs. Although he could have flourished in any of these fields for a lifetime, something mysterious still called him.

One fascination which did not fit easily into Schweitzer's life was the statue of a Congolese man by Frédéric-Auguste Bartholdi (who also sculpted the Statue of Liberty) in the town square of Colmar, Germany. Photos of the statue, which was deliberately destroyed by the Nazis near the end of World War II, show a handsome, muscular, and very thoughtful man leaning back against a pillar. "His face with its sad, thoughtful expression spoke to me of the misery of the Dark Continent," Schweitzer wrote, referring to the cruelty that white people had inflicted on Africans.[3] Schweitzer was so moved by the pain and dignity in the statue that he made excuses to go to Colmar and hold imaginary conversations with the statue.

Near his thirtieth birthday, Schweitzer saw an article about the need for medical help in Africa. Immediately, he knew he was called to become a doctor and serve there. Soon he realized he was also called to build a clinic and support it through writing and organ concerts.

In the sound-bite version, only the flash of insight, "I am called to be a doctor in Africa and build a hospital" is told. In the fuller story, the vision has many roots, especially the patient habits of walking questions into daily life and paying attention to fascinations, however unusual. Critical to these habits is the attitude of embracing mysterious things that don't fit—even those things that irritate—for they often herald one's growing edge, one's potential pearl of great wisdom.

In the story of the of the Post-it Note ™ in chapter 2, there was evidence of how playfully creativity can work individually and in teams. In the stories of Schweitzer, we can see the power of creativity that is deliberately grounded into deep ethical values. In the stories throughout this book, we see many ways that spirit and creativity can create everyday work-life excellence.

Together these stories offer a series of questions that may help you tap your visionary potentials for the highest, deepest, and broadest good:

- How can I "walk"questions into my life and work?
- How can I learn to embrace "mistakes" or "failures" as part of my creative process?
- How can nature show me the way toward meaningful and satisfying work?
- How can I develop persistence to follow ideas until they are ethically implemented?
- How can I best tap into and learn from religious and spiritual traditions in shaping my core values?
- How can I practice my basic values in a way that inspires others?

Ingredients and Guidelines for Envisioning Ethical and Meaningful Work

From a small business I'll call Joe's Car Wash comes a simple model for creating businesses and institutions that are financially successful while being meaningful, ethical, and satisfying. What makes Joe's Car Wash successful is the way Joe has blended four basic visioning ingredients:

One part dreaming: a combination of many powerful essences: imagination, the courage to go beyond what is already known or approved, and a doorway to your deepest values. Joe first developed his dreamer consciousness when he was stuck in an unsatisfying job and imagined owning his own business. Now he uses his creativity in his marketing efforts as he dreams of an expanded business.

One part hobby consciousness: doing things just because they are fun to do. Joe is like a kid who never lost his excitement over cars. His passion for cars is contagious to customers, who appreciate the fact that he loves the exercise he gets from polishing cars, and he loves seeing cars turn from grime to shine.

One part mission or calling: something you do because it matters greatly to you, including creating change in the world. Joe feels called to help people maintain their cars in beautiful condition for a fair price. He loves helping people develop great work habits and fulfill their own business dreams. He also loves having money to give back to the community.

One part pragmatic business sense: the determination to do whatever is necessary to provide excellent service and to receive a fair return (profit or wages) for the expenditure of time, money, and other resources. For business owners, this also includes the willingness to risk these resources without any guarantee of return. For Joe, creating a successful business requires giving up Saturday morning basketball games with buddies and learning how to become an efficient manager.

As in Southern cooking recipes, there are no specific amounts for any ingredients or a set formula for creating a vision. However, here are some guidelines:

- Without dreaming, we get stuck in a limited, unsatisfying reality. We fail to see our heart's desire, and we ignore options or resources that could help turn vision into reality. With too much or distorted wishful thinking, we can become grandiose or dissatisfied with what's possible.[4]

- Without hobby consciousness, we lack joy and zest for ourselves, our customers, staff, and others. With too much or distorted hobby consciousness, the work doesn't get done well.

- Without a mission or calling, we fail to do work that feels purposeful or that matters to others. When the mission is distorted or overwhelming, we may burn ourselves out. Either we work without expecting to be paid enough for our efforts, or we expect others to fund us. We might also become preachy or pushy.

- Without enough pragmatic business consciousness, we may have fun and help others, but we will soon wear ourselves out and/or go broke.

With balance, we can create a job or business that reflects our talents, needs, limitations, and gifts. We have fun while serving a useful purpose that matters to us. We build a business or career with a bottom line of integrity that reaps financial and other rewards.

The basic business plan outline, which is available free from any Small Business Administration office and most banks that offer small business loans, can be adapted to a spiritual business plan.[5] To develop a viable plan, business owners have to think through questions such as Who is my target market? How can I reach this market? Why would customers choose my goods and services over those of a competitor? What do I need to do to receive a great ROI (return on investment)?

The business plan outline is designed to be answered primarily by the pragmatic business consciousness. Here are some sample questions that invite your other consciousnesses to the planning table:

Dreamer: When I imagine opening a letter from a satisfied customer, what do I imagine the letter says? If I were to open a letter from the daughter of an employee saying she is so glad her daddy works for me, what would that letter say?

Hobby: How can I bring more fun and satisfaction into the process of keeping the books? Hiring and training employees? Doing inventory?

Mission: How can I measure return on investment so it includes all costs (e.g., my company's impact on the earth and on the lives of my employees) and benefits (the good we do in the larger community and the satisfaction we obtain from being in business)? How can we create a financially successful business with a bottom line of integrity?

Envisioning a Promised Land

That word *integrity* keeps popping up, as well it should. The world is always enriched when we use our creative capacities for the good, and it is diminished when we would use these capacities in the service of our pride, self-will, or fear.

Once again, integrity is about much more than being honest and ethical. It is about being true to ourselves, even when we are lost or in pain. In Walter Brueggemann's *Prophetic Imagination*,[6] the symbolism of the Exodus becomes a metaphor for what gives people the courage to make big changes. The people of Exodus have the memory of God's goodness, which led them to believe that they could continue to rely on God. In the present was their awareness of the pain of oppression and the belief that the oppression would continue if they stayed where they were. For the future, they had a vision of the promised land.

Barbara Valuckas, SSND (School Sisters of Notre Dame), uses this metaphor and many other types of visioning processes to help members of Catholic congregations create compelling images that can guide them into a meaningful future. Driving her work are studies showing that religious orders have only a brief window of opportunity to re-vision themselves or they will decline without attracting new members. "We don't have time to piddle around about questions of meaning. We have to rearticulate meaning for the postmodern age in which we live. Because the future exists only in the imagination, there needs to be an image of the future that's compelling enough to counter oppression and resistance in the present."

One of Sister Barbara's concerns is that women religious are becoming so involved in daily parish activities that they are losing their prophetic edge. One correlation for secular work, according to Sister Barbara, is that

> . . . In every person's life are stretch points. In psychological terms, this is called the growing edge. It's hard to retain that prophetic edge when you are employed full-time. One thing religious congregations have going for them is that they already have some common values and common goals. They have an articulated mission and, though they wonder what it means for the future, they know why they are on earth.[7]

With care, work and its challenges can be a catalyst for discovering our mission on earth. Roberto Vargas, an organizational development consultant and visionary strategist, says:

> We live in a time that is pregnant with thoughts and possibilities. We all are more conscious of how we are connected with others throughout the world. Every day is precious, for we know now that each time we speak with others, it may be our last. We're rethinking what it means to be in the world, to be American, to be secure. We know we need more justice. What's important for all of us now is to step up and recognize that we are all called to be leaders. As we look to the future, we also need to draw from the ancestors.[8]

Vargas is excited that a tradition from his heritage, the Dia de los Muertos, or Day of the Dead, has taken root in American culture.[9] "From the ancestors we draw spiritual support and guidance. We need to hold on to their visions and hopes, and let them inspire us."

We can also invite those of the future, including the men and women we are becoming, to guide and inspire us.

Visiting Your Future of Meaningful and Joyous Work

At the beginning of this book, we looked at the image of, on the one hand, meaning, on the other hand, work. As we prepare to end with resources for your journey, let your imagination carry you into a future filled with meaningful and joyous work for yourself and others.

What dreams do you have for your own job? For your company or profession?

Imagine you and some colleagues are talking about how much more satisfying everyone's work is in the future. What specific things do you say to each other? What stories do you imagine telling each other about how you created more meaningful and satisfying work?

Imagine that, as you are sharing your wonderful stories, someone joins you. Way back when you first started to read this book, that person was on your list of difficult people; now he or she is a cherished colleague. What do you imagine made the difference?

Imagine that you of the present meet you of the future. Imagine that Future You says, "Thank you. Thank you for daring to dream that work could be more meaningful and joyous. Thank you for helping me create work that is more ethical, more creative, more rewarding."

Finally, remembering that Future You is always present in your imagination, come back to the present and begin your journey of creating work with meaning, work with joy right here, right now.

10

Resources for Meaningful and Satisfying Work

This chapter could easily become a thick book. In selecting the resources, the following criteria were used:

* Will the resources help individuals and small groups to work more meaningfully and joyfully?[1]
* Are the resources ecumenical in nature, hospitable to other faiths, or models for practices that can be adapted to other faiths?
* Do the resources complement or extend the themes in this book?

Special attention was paid to resources that are free or available online, as well as resources that are not well known. Hopefully, these resources will give you new appreciation for the many ways people now enjoy meaningful work, and will spur your own creativity and research.

Comprehensive "Don't Miss" Resources

Association for Spirit at Work, founded by Judi Neal, who created the website www.spiritatwork.com and has been "information central" for the spirit and work movement for more than seven years. Check here for information and connections including:

* articles (including archived "Spirit and Work" newsletters; books, and links);

- conferences and special events throughout the world;
- courses at the university and graduate level, textbooks and course syllabi;
- current research and an archive of research papers; local chapters throughout the world.

Bringing Your Soul to Work: An Everyday Practice by Cheryl Peppers and Alan Briskin. Practical wisdom for people in any field. While gentle in tone, the book offers an unflinching (and often neglected) call to face the shadow side of self and others (San Francisco: Berrett-Koehler, 2000).

Centre for Spirituality and Work in Toronto. Even if you never plan to visit Toronto, consider getting on their contact list at www.spiritualityatwork.org. This very active center presents outstanding conferences and workshops that draw people from all backgrounds. Its archive of events is a gold mine of ideas for designing programs in your area.

Heart at Work: Stories and Strategies for Building Self-Esteem and Reawakening the Soul at Work, edited by Jack Canfield and Jacqueline Miller (New York: McGraw Hill, 1996), and *Chicken Soup for the Soul at Work: 101 Stories of Compassion and Creativity in the Workplace*, edited by Jack Canfield, Mark Victor Hansen, Maida Rogerson, Martin Rutte, and Tim Clauss (Deerfield Beach, FL: Health Communications, 1996). These books are useful even in firms where the word *spirituality* seems anathema. They also provide insights for clergy, therapists, and vocational counselors about workplace issues. See also www.martinrutte.com for basic, nonthreatening articles and guidelines for working with stories at work.

The Reinvention of Work: A New Vision of Livelihood for Our Time by Matthew Fox. A passionate and lively reframing of how we see work that's firmly rooted in history and the world's religious and mystical traditions (San Francisco: Harper Collins, 1994).

The response to this book caused Fox to create a Doctoral of Ministry program that is focused on bringing spirituality and the new cosmology to reinventing work. More than four hundred students from all professions have enrolled in the past four years (about seventy graduated): engineers, doctors, social workers, therapists, educators, health care professionals, clergy, artists, activists, businesspeople, lawyers. For information go to www.creationspirituality.org.

"A Spiritual Pilgrimage to Corporate America: A Report of a Sabbatical Study on Spirituality and Business Organisations" by British Industrial chaplain David Welbourn. Reports of interviews with CEOs, theologians, and authors in fall 2000, followed by theological implications, bibliography, and appendices (including Mike Bell's great satire on the reasons managers fear spirit and work). Available free from david@dwelbourn.freeserve.co.uk.

Spirituality at Work is a great starting place to understand spirit and work in the context of all traditions (www.Spiritualityatwork.com). The site offers selections from Whitney Roberson's beautifully researched "Spirituality at Work: A Handbook for Conversation Convenors and Facilitators."

Transforming Practices: How to Find Joy and Satisfaction in the Legal Life by Steven Keeva (sponsored by the *ABA Journal*, Chicago: Contemporary Books, 1998). One of the very best practical books on spirit and work for people of any field, this book offers insights on how to integrate such spiritual practices as the Benedictine Rule, yoga, or contemplative prayer into professional work. Keeva's website (www.transformingpractices.com) contains articles, book excerpts, interviews, and exercises that live up to the book's title.

Various online resources for meditation, contemplative prayer, and monastic practices that can be used well in workplaces include:

- www.Digiserve.com/mystic: resources and links from many mystical traditions (Buddhism, Christianity, Judaism, Hinduism, Islam, Taoism)
- Douai Abbey (a British Benedictine abbey) offers regular retreats on contemplative prayer and spirituality in business. See the article on spirit and work by Fr. Dermot Tredget on the abbey's website at www.members.aol.com/douaiweb/faithbus.htm
- High Tor Alliance (www.hightor.org) offers reports on various types of contemplative prayer at work
- *Spiritual Exercises of St. Ignatius of Loyola* as translated from his autobiography by Elder Mullan, SF, available at www.ccel.org/i/ignatius/exercises

Websites www.beliefnet.com, www.spiritualityhealth.com, and www.about.com offer outstanding brief links to all religions, as well as articles and columns (often by internationally known authors) about practical spirituality.

Resources Keyed to Chapter Themes

Preface
Exploring a New World of Spirit at Work

Articles
Articles about spirituality and work, once rare, can now be found in most major magazines. Many of these articles can be found online through www.findarticles.com or through a specific magazine's website.

"Creating an Inspiring Workplace" by Carole Schweitzer, *Association Management*, July 1998.

"God and Business" by Marc Gunther, *Fortune Magazine*, July 2001.

"God and the CEO: Does Spirituality belong in the Board-room?" by Jim Braham, *Industry Week*, February 1, 1999.

"Religion in the Workplace: The Growing Presence of Spiri-tuality in Corporate America" by Michelle Conlin. *Business Week*, November 1, 1999.

"The Soul at Work." A comprehensive special section of the *Los Angeles Times Business Section*, April 6, 1998. Its more than a dozen practical articles make this well worth a trip to your library's microfilm section.

Books

The Next American Spirituality: Finding God in the 21st Century by Tim Jones and George Gallup, Jr. A thoughtful and com-prehensive look at how a large group of Americans actually acted in regard to spirituality during a forty-eight-hour period (Colorado Springs, CO: Chariot Victor, 2000).

Shopping for Faith: American Religion in the New Millennium by Richard Cimino and Don Lattin. Gives a much needed con-text for searching for self and spirit, community, and com-mon culture (San Francisco: Jossey-Bass, 1998).

A Spiritual Audit of Corporate America: A Hard Look at Spiritu-ality, Religion, and Values in the Workplace by Ian I. Mitroff and Elizabeth A. Denton. Results from the first-ever survey of spiritual beliefs and practices among U.S. managers and executives that found: 1) most workers had strong beliefs yet believed it was not okay to act on them yet; 2) companies in which spiritual and company values coalesce are more suc-cessful (San Francisco: Jossey-Bass, 1999).

Magazines and Newsletters

Business Spirit Journal. Online magazine with articles on many topics by leaders in the field (www.bizspirit.com). Each issue features an excerpt from Stanley Herman's *The Tao at Work: On Leading and Following* (San Francisco: Jossey-Bass, 1994).

Faith in Business Quarterly. A joint publication by the Ridley Hall Foundation and the Industrial Christian Fellowship in the United Kingdom relates Christian and ecumenical values to the business world (www.fibq.org).

Organizations, Special Projects, and List Serves

Business for Social Responsibility helps companies integrate commercial success with ethical values, people, communities, and the environment. 609 Mission Street, 2nd Floor, San Francisco, CA 94105-3506; 415-537-0888 (www.bsr.org).

Center for Visionary Leadership (www.visionarylead.org) offers new models for integrating spirituality and politics. It has co-sponsored conferences on spirit and work.

Heartland Institute has sponsored several conferences on spirit and work and now promotes Thought Leader gatherings (www.heartlandinstitute.com).

Presidio Dialogues are monthly dialogues on various spirit and work themes held at the Presidio in San Francisco (www.renesch.com/presidio).

Shalem Organization (www.shalem.org) is a spiritual direction and resource center in Washington, D.C. Their Soul of the Executive Program is extensive, and its application form is a great source for discussion questions. *Shalem News OnLine* contains articles by Shalem founder Tilden Edwards, Gerald May, and others.

Spiritual Sisters of the Internet Café's spirituality and work section offers stories on leadership, balance, time, meaning, and other topics (www.spiritualsisters.com/business.htm).

www.wisdomnetwork.com offers radio and television shows about meaningful life and work. Columns include Marsha Sinetar on vocation and John Renesch on conscious leadership.

Worklife Institute, 7100 Regency Square, Suite 210, Houston, TX 77036, and Institute of WorkLife Ministry (www.worklifeministry.com) offer educational programs in mediation, counseling, and life work issues. Links to the National Institute of Business and Industrial Chaplains.

Human Resources, Leadership, and Legal Issues of Spirit and Work

Multiple articles: search by keywords on www.fastcompany.com and www.workforce.com.

"Religion and Spirituality in the Workplace—Do You Know Your Rights?" by Michael Thompson. At www.workforce.com /archive/article/22/08/08/php.

"Workplace Guideposts: Which forms of religious expression are acceptable on the job and which are not? Here are some unofficial rules" by Melinda Fulmer, *Los Angeles Times*, April 6, 1998, in the special section "Soul at Work."

Chapter One
Discovering New Possibilities for Meaning and Joy at Work

"Better Workplace" (www.betterworkplacenow.com) is a website based on Tom Terez's *22 Keys to a Better Workplace*. It offers excerpts from the book, explanations, and exercises. The site's numerous articles include some that are as funny as they are wise. (Terez is a columnist for *Workforce Magazine*.)

Love the Work You're With: Find the Job You Always Wanted without Leaving the One You Have by Richard C. Whiteley. Well researched and easily readable tools for transforming your work—even if your organization does not change (New York: Henry Holt, 2001).

Man's Search for Meaning (Boston: Beacon: 1992) and *The Unheard Cry for Meaning* (Old Tappan, NJ: Simon & Schuster, 1978) by Viktor Frankl are the cornerstones of logotherapy, or a psychology based on our inbred will to meaning.

The Power of Purpose: Creating Meaning in Your Life and Work by Richard J. Leider. An often-quoted book on how to use your talents purposefully in a mission greater than yourself. For individual and group use (San Francisco: Berrett-Koehler, 1997).

The Search for Meaning in the Workplace by Thomas H. Naylor, William H. Willimon, and Rolf Osterberg. Practical philosophy with wonderful examples and quotes from the world of business and law (Nashville, TN: Abingdon Press, 1996).

The Way of Adventure: Transforming Your Life and Work with Spirit and Vision by Jeff Salz. Stories and tips for living in the moment while following longtime challenges. Salz finds more excitement in everyday life and work than he once found while scaling the world's most dangerous and highest peaks (New York: John Wiley & Sons, 2000).

True Work: Doing What You Love and Loving What You Do by Michael Toms and Justine Willis Toms. A wise and witty guide and storybook from the founders of New Dimensions Radio. Great discussion group resource (New York: Bell Tower, 1998).

What Does It Mean to Be Human? Reverence for Life Reaffirmed by Responses from around the World. Several hundred thoughtful responses gathered by Frederick Franck, Janis Roze, and Richard Connolly (Nyack, NY: Circumstantial Publishing, in cooperation with UNESCO, 1998).

www.ForgivenessNet.co.uk. Stories, articles, insights, and religious scriptures about the meaning and power of forgiveness, human and divine.

Chapter Two
Seeing Your Work as a Spiritual Journey

A Call for Connection: Solutions for Creating a Whole New Culture by Gail Bernice Holland. Hopeful, resource-filled documentation of how people throughout the world are changing the world in many fields (Novato, CA: New World Library, 1998).

Compassion in Action: Setting Out on the Path of Service by Ram Dass and Mirabai Bush. How to be more attentive and responsive to the suffering of others (New York: Bell Tower Books, 1992).

Depression and the Body: The Biological Basis for Faith and Reality by Alexander Lowen. A classic text on how the body carries our ego defenses, which then affect energy, and how we view the world. Even though Lowen rarely uses the word *spiritual*, it is profoundly so (New York: Viking Paperback, 1993).

Dr. Marcia Emery's Intuition Workbook: An Expert's Guide to Unlocking the Wisdom of Your Subconscious Mind by Marcia Emery. This well-organized workbook includes sections on centering, receptivity, interpreting images, and achieving mental clarity (Upper Saddle River, NJ: Prentice Hall, 1994).

Drawing on the Right Side of the Brain by Betty Edwards. Recommended for anyone who is ready to see the world more acutely and from new perspectives. Fun and provocative (New York: Tarcher Books, 1979).

Greenleaf Center (greenleaf.org). Based on the work of Robert Greenleaf, who is often cited as the guiding elder of the current spirit and work movement. Greenleaf offers networking, resources, and information about servant leadership.

Holy Work: Be Love, Be Blessed, Be a Blessing by Marsha Sinetar (New York: Crossroad Pub. Co., 1998). This is the latest book on work by the author of *Do What You Love, the Money Will Follow,* which is credited with transforming the vocational consulting field and popularizing the concept of right livelihood.

"If You Do What You Love, Will the Money Follow? The Path to 'Right Livelihood' Requires More Than Self-Confidence or Enthusiasm: It Takes Honesty, Commitment and Hard Work" by D. Patrick Miller. Sobering and inspiring (*Yoga Journal,* May/June 1990).

Jump Start Your Brain by Doug Hall. Fun ways to get ideas flying in groups (literally and figuratively). Although totally secular, the book's exercises work well in spiritual contexts (New York: Warner Books, 1995).

Living Your Life Out Loud: How to Unlock Your Creativity and Unleash Your Joy by Salli Raspberry and Padi Selwyn. Open to any page in this book and you'll find great stories, great attitude, great consciousness (New York: Pocket Books, 1981).

Money and the Meaning of Life by Jacob Needleman. How understanding money helps us understand ourselves and how to bring spiritual wisdom to everyday challenges (New York: Doubleday, 1994).

Money Harmony: Resolving Money Conflicts in Your Life and Your Relationships by Olivia Mellan. Determining your money patterns (hoarding, spending, avoiding dealing with it, and feeling guilt about having anything); how you developed these patterns and how to transcend them so money supports rather than undermines relationships and well-being (New York: Walker & Co., 1995).

No Enemies Within: A Creative Process for Discovering What's Right about What's Wrong by Dawna Markova. How to turn "heartbreaks into breakthroughs, and internal enemies into allies," by a gifted teacher and therapist (Berkeley, CA: Conari Press, 1988).

No Place to Hide: Facing Shame So We Can Find Self-Respect by Michael P. Nichols. How to heal toxic shame or guilt; how to heed productive calls to act with more integrity in work and life (New York: Simon & Schuster, 1991).

Social Service Websites include: Business for Social Responsibility (www.bsr.org); *Business Ethics* magazine (www.business-ethics.com); The Metaphor Project (www.metaphorproject.org); Social Venture Network (www.svn.org); Sojourners organization and magazine (www.sojo.net); Tikkun (www.Tikkun.org, and United for a Fair Economy (www.ufenet.org).

SQ: Connecting with Our Spiritual Intelligence by Dana Zohar and Ian Marshall (New York: Bloomsbury, 2001). Look in your bookstore for other titles on the subject of spiritual intelligence.

Stone Soup for the World: Life Changing Stories of Kindness and Courageous Acts of Service, edited by Marianne Larned. How to make a huge difference by taking simple actions with great love (Berkeley, CA: Conari Press, 1997).

Taking Back Our Lives in the Age of Corporate Dominance by Ellen Schwartz and Suzanne Stoddard. Living authentically in an often-scary, frenetic world while integrating personal and social issues; great resource section (San Francisco: Berrett-Koehler, 2000).

The Artist's Way: A Spiritual Path to Creativity by Julia Cameron. Filled with exercises and stories on how to rediscover your most authentic and healthy self (Los Angeles: Tarcher Books, 1992). Also see Cameron's *The Vein of Gold: A Journey to Your Creative Heart* (Los Angeles: Tarcher Books, 1996).

The Blessing by Gary Smalley and John Trent. Rooted in biblical teachings, this book provides a new perspective and appreciation for the importance of blessing in everyday interactions and relationships (Nashville, TN: T. Nelson Pocket Books, 1986).

The Call by David Spangler. How divine love is interpreted through various traditions; our need to listen carefully so we can know who we are and what we are called to do (New York: Riverhead Books, 1992).

The Courage to Create by Rollo May. The classic text on the nature of creativity, why we fear it, and how true courage is linked to the heart (New York: Norton Bantam, 1975).

The Hero Within: Six Archetypes We Live By by Carol S. Pearson. Marvelous introduction to Jungian archetypes and myths that can either control or guide us (San Francisco: Harper & Row, be sure to get any edition of 1986 or after, which include exercises for working with each archetype).

The Hero's Journey: Joseph Campbell on His Life and Work by Joseph Campbell. This book is the excellent companion to the documentary on the same name, which aired on PBS along with Bill Moyers's acclaimed six-part series, *Joseph Campbell and the Power of Myth*. The videos are available in most libraries and video stores.

The Other 90%: How to Unlock Your Vast Untapped Potential for Leadership & Life by Robert K. Cooper. Motivation, stories, and practical tools, including recent research on the wisdom of our three brains (head, heart, and gut) (New York: Crown Business, 2001).

The Undefended Self: Living the Pathwork of Spiritual Wholeness by Susan Thesenga. Stories and tools for daring to unmask the games and belief systems that prevent us from facing the worst in ourselves and liberating our gifts (Madison, VA: Pathwork Press, 1994).

The Zen of Seeing: Seeing/Drawing as Meditation by Frederick Franck (New York: Random House, 1973). This recently re-issued classic is the first of Franck's inspiring art-as-meditation books. In his nineties, Franck is still writing, drawing, sculpting.

What Color Is Your Parachute? A Practical Manual for Job-Hunters and Career Changers by Richard Bolles. This perennial best-seller has great resources for people who love their jobs but want to know more about themselves (Berkeley, CA: Ten Speed Press, 2001).

Your Money or Your Life: Transforming Your Relationship with Money and Achieving Financial Independence by Joe Dominguez and Vicki Robin. How and why to measure the true cost of everything we buy in relationship to the value it brings; living from deeper values (New York: Penguin USA, 1999).

Chapter Three
Creating and Using a Workplace Altar

All About Altars by Lama Surya Dass. A Buddhist perspective on altar building. Available at www.beliefnet.com.

Altars Made Easy: A Complete Guide to Creating Your Own Sacred Space by Peg Streep. The best-known book of its kind, with information on altar design, altar cloths, statuary, etc. (San Francisco: HarperSanFrancisco, 1997).

Black Pearls: Daily Meditations, Affirmations and Inspirations for African-Americans, compiled by Eric V. Copage. The words of Martin Luther King Jr., Rosa Parks, Alice Walker, etc. offer moving ways to start the day (New York: Quill, 1993).

Earth Prayers from Around the World: 365 Prayers,Poems, and Invocations for Honoring the Earth, edited by Elizabeth Roberts and Elias Amidon. Prayers, poetry, and thoughts for contemplation from all spiritual traditions (San Francisco: HarperSanFrancisco, 1991).

Every Eye Beholds You: A World Treasury of Prayer, edited by Thomas J. Craughwell with introduction by Karen Armstrong. Prayers for all purposes that give you a wonderful introduction to the unity and unique wisdom of traditions from many centuries (New York: Harcourt Brace, 1998).

Illuminating God's House by Vanessah Ochs. Discusses altar building from a Torah perspective. Available at www.beliefnet.com.

In the Spirit by *Essence Magazine* Editor Susan L. Taylor. A collection of Taylor's monthly columns, which often are copied and passed among friends (New York: Amistad Publishers, 1994).

Mystics, Masters, Saints and Sages: Stories of Enlightenment, edited by Robert Ullman and Judyth Reichenberg-Ullman with forward by the Dalai Lama (Berkeley, CA: Conari Press, 2001).

Ordinary Graces: Christian Teachings on the Interior Life, edited by Lorraine Kisly with introduction by Philip Zaleski (New York: Bell Tower, 2000).

Sacred Space: Clearing and Enhancing the Energy of Your Home by Denise Lin. Based on research from multiple traditions (New York: Ballantine, 1996).

The View of an Open Heart by Brad Olsen. Basic insights on sacred space at www.spiritualityhealth.com.

The Way We Pray: Prayer Practices around the World, edited by Maggie Oman Shannon with foreward by Dean Alan Jones (Berkeley, CA: Conari Press, 2001).

Walking a Sacred Path: Rediscovering the Labyrinth as a Spiritual Path by Lauren Artress. A priest at Grace Cathedral in San Francisco who has most prominently promoted this ancient meditation practice (New York: Riverhead, 1996).

Chapter Four
Turning Stress and Burnout into Energy and Insight

Aikido is a spiritually grounded martial art. There are many books on the subject. Among the websites on the subject are www.bodymindandmodem.com.

Beverly Potter (www.docpotter.com) offers burnout assessments, plus very practical short articles on how to deal with specific burnout problems

Grieving the Death of a Friend by Harold Ivan Smith. Poetry, stories, and information on how to deal with the loss of a friend and keep on living (or working) (Minneapolis: Augsburg Fortress, 1995).

Living in Balance: A Dynamic Approach for Creating Harmony and Wholeness in a Chaotic World by Joel Levey and Michelle Levey. A synthesis of ancient mindfulness practices with cutting-edge research on peak human performance (Berkeley, CA: Conari Press, 1998).

Managing to Have Fun by Matt Weinstein. Begins with a beautiful description of the spirit of fun, then continues with examples and stories on how and why to bring play to work (New York: Fireside, 1997). The website www.playfair.com has more ideas on team building and stress release through fun.

Stopping: How to Be Still When You Have to Keep Going by David Jundtz with foreward by Richard Carlson. Finding the serene still-points inside busy lives (Berkeley, CA: Conari Press, 1998).

"Stress and Burnout in Ministry" by Rowland Croucher, churchlink.com.au/forum/r_croucher/stress_burnout.html. A focused, witty piece that is useful to all in helping professions.

The Balancing Act free newsletter from Alan Weiss, available at www.summitconsulting.com.

The Fun Nun, Sister Mary Christelle Macaluso: This Sister of Mercy's mission includes bringing the healing power of laughter to the workplace. For several articles on the power of humor, see www.speakers-podium.com/funnun.

The Heartmath Solution by Doc Childre and Howard Martin with Donna Beech. Practical tools for turning anxiety and stress into emotional clarity, creativity, and improved health. Chapters on care vs. overcare are especially useful for those who burn out from giving too much to others (San Francisco: HarperSanFrancisco, 1999).

The Simple Living Guide: A Sourcebook for Less Stressful, More Joyful Living by former attorney Janet Luhrs. A thick and comprehensive meaningful living and working sourcebook (New York: Broadway Books, 1997).

"Work as Play" by Robert Rabbin. A brief article focusing on the power of enthusiasm, freedom, truth, and devotion. Available at www.robrabbin.com/wisdomatwork.html.

Zen Computer: Mindfulness and the Machine by Philip Toshio Sudo. Mindfulness techniques playfully presented for people who may not now enjoy working with computers (New York: Simon & Schuster, 1999).

Chapter Five
Finding Wisdom for Work from Many Traditions

Institute on Ecumenical and Cultural Research (www.iecr.org). The site has great links for other groups and magazines.

Religion and Ethics Newsweekly. A weekly PBS program focusing on news from all faiths. The website offers a viewers guide and suggestions for discussion groups (www.pbs.org/wnet/religionandethics).

The Illustrated World's Religions: A guide to Our Wisdom Traditions by Huston Smith. Exquisitely illustrated, beautifully written, this book combines childlike awe with years of scholarly research and a lifetime of experiencing how others see God (San Francisco: HarperSanFrancisco, 1994). For an interview with Dr. Smith about the world's religions and work, see www.visionary-resources.com.

The World's Wisdom: Sacred Texts of the World's Religions, edited by Philip Novak with foreward by Huston Smith. Selections from the seven major religions as well as from primal religions throughout the world (San Francisco: HarperSanFrancisco, 1994).

United World Religions is building interfaith communities modeled after the United Nations. Their website, www.united-religions.org, offers numerous interfaith materials and links.

Chapter Six
Tapping Your Own Wisdom throughout the Workday

Awake My Soul: Practical Spirituality for Busy People by Timothy Jones. Twelve practices for being in tune with and directed by that which matters most (New York: Doubleday, 1984).

Breath Walk: Breathing Your Way to a Revitalized Body, Mind and Spirit by Gurucharan Singh Khalsa and Yogi Bhajan. Simple walking and kundalini yoga meditations are combined to integrate body, mind, and spirit (New York: Broadway Books, 2000).

Corporate Mystic: A Guide for Visionaries with Their Feet on the Ground by Gay Hendricks and Kate Ludeman. A popular guide to gaining wisdom at work (New York: Bantam, 1997).

Let Your Life Speak: Listening for the voice of Vocation by Parker J. Palmer. A guide to hearing the most authentic voice of wisdom within and without by a respected Quaker teacher (San Francisco: Jossey-Bass, 2000).

Receiving the Day: Christian Practices for Opening the Gift of Time by Dorothy C. Bass. How to heal our relationship with time through stories, ancient practices, and in-the-moment presence (San Francisco: Jossey-Bass, 2000).

Simple Meditation & Relaxation by Joel Levey and Michelle Levey. Going way beyond ordinary stress release, the book offers discernment questions that are recommended for meditation and spiritual support group members (Berkeley, CA: Conari Press, 1999).

Solved by Sunset: The Right Brain Way to Resolve Whatever's Bothering You in One Day or Less by Carol Orsborn. A much more prophetic book than the subtitle suggests (New York: Harmony Books, 1995).

Spirituality@Work: 10 Ways to Balance Your Life On-the-Job by Gregory F. A. Pierce with forword from Mark Hostetter. Ten disciplines for putting spiritual teachings into practice based on e-mail conversations among hundreds of business people (Chicago: Loyola Press, 2001).

Work as a Spiritual Practice: A Practical Buddhist Approach to Inner Growth and Satisfaction on the Job by Lewis Richmond. How to use commute time, worry, and other everyday stresses as preludes to wisdom (New York: Broadway Books, 1999).

Chapter Seven
Working with Integrity as Your Bottom Line

Be Heard Now: Tap into Your Inner Speaker and Communicate with Your Inner Speaker and Communicate with Ease by Lee

Glickstein. Recommended for anyone, public speaker or not. Includes instructions on how to create a "speaking circle" in which peers support each other to develop personal authenticity (New York: Broadway Books, 1998).

Bio-spirituality: Focusing as a Way to Grow by Peter A. Campbell and Edwin M. McMahon. Judeo-Christian and Jungian insights that help readers to know more about their real selves while connecting with that which is beyond self (Chicago: Loyola University Press, 1995).

EarthLight Magazine, which focuses on spirituality and ecology, offers many articles online through its website (www.earthlight.org).

"Ethical Dilemmas — Then and Now" by Brenda Paik Suno in the January 1, 1997 *Workforce Magazine.* An overview of the main HR ethical questions of the past eighty years. Available online at www.workforce.com.

European Business Ethics Network (www.eben.org). Business people and academics who promote debate and exchange of information through conferences and a quarterly newsletter. Great links to ethics organizations throughout the world.

Foundation for Ethics and Meaning (www.meaning.org). Offers insight into meaningful politics beyond left or right paradigms, including the online newsletter, "Meaning Matters."

Reconciliation and Healing Service between Victims of Clergy Abuse and the Roman Catholic Diocese of Oakland: A moving model for those who need to apologize for any wrongdoing or for not stopping the wrongdoing of others. http://www.oakdiocese.org/reconcile-contents.htm. See also the diocese's policies on dealing with sexual abuse by clergy at www.oakdiocese/survivors.

Stirring the Waters: Writing to Find Your Spirit. Poetic and practical guidance about how to use various writing practices to discover what's in your heart and soul (Boston: Tuttle Publishing, 2001).

The Dancing Animal Woman: A Celebration of Life by Anne Hillman. One woman's radical transformation from fast-track trainer to vital woman who is awed by the universe (Norfolk, CT: Bramble Books, 1994).

Whistleblower support organizations: Government Accountability Project (GAP, at www.whistleblower.org) and National Whistleblowers Center (www.whistleblowers.org) both offer comprehensive advice to those who dare confront fraud, waste, and abuse at work. The website of Donald Soeken, an expert on the unique stress and needs of whistleblowers, can be accessed at www.purespeed.com/personal/helpine or through the GAP site.

Writing for Your Life: A Guide and Companion to the Inner Voice by Deena Metzger. Using writing as a path to healing, self-revelation, growth, and spiritual path (San Francisco: HarperSan Francisco, 1992).

Chapter Eight
Creating Spiritual Community at and for Your Work

Appreciative Inquiry. See "A Dialogue about Leadership and Appreciative Inquiry" by Marjorie Schiller and other articles at www.sol-wc.org.

Business Storytellers provide information on the importance of stories, guidelines, and resources, as well as notes from storytellers on varied workplace topics at www.bizstorytellers.org.

Wisdom Circles: A Guide to Self-Discovery and Community Building in Small Groups by Charles Garfield, Cindy Spring, and Sedonia Cahill. Why and how to create and work with ceremonial circles that invoke the wisdom of each member (New York: Hyperion, 1998).

Chapter Nine
Envisioning and Re-Visioning your Work
and your Profession

"Are You Holding You Back?" by Sandy Boucher from the April 1995 *Writer's Digest* is one of the best-ever articles on how to liberate creativity. Available online at www.sandy-boucher.com

Chaordic Alliance (www.chaotic.org), founded by Dee Hock, creator of VISA, seeks to create visionary business through sharing research, ideas, and resources. (The word *chaordic* combines "chaos" and "order.") The site has great articles and links.

Creating by Robert Fritz. Grounded visionary skill-building practices from a master composer, creative consultant, and caring teacher (New York: Fawcett Columbine, 1991).

Creativity in Business by Michael Ray and Rochelle Meyers. Based on a revolutionary Stanford University course. Stories from transformative businesses with exercises to liberate creativity quickly. The hieroglyphics exercise alone is worth the price of the book (New York: Doubleday, 1989).

Getting to a Better Future: A Matter of Conscious Choosing by John Renesch and Anita Roddick. An optimistic book from two realists who have been working with spiritual principles in business for many years (San Francisco: New Business Books, 2000).

Guide to Liberating Your Soul (Alexandria, VA: Fulfilling Books, 1995) and *Liberating the Corporate Soul: Building a Visionary Organization* (Woburn, MA: Butterworth Heinemann, 1998) by Richard Barrett. Processes for personal and organizational growth that draw on leading-edge theories of science, religion, and psychology, by the founder of a spirit and work discussion group at the World Bank.

Imaginization: New Mindsets for Seeing, Organizing and Managing. Practical and fun tools for helping an organization be more imaginative and better able to meet changing marketplace conditions. Great graphics and metaphors make it easy to grasp and communicate the book's key concepts (San Francisco: Berrett-Koehler, 1997).

Institute of Noetic Sciences (www.ions.org). A leader in the field of consciousness and human potential research and education for more than twenty-five years. A membership organization with great publications and meetings.

Law and the Heart: A Practical Guide for Successful Lawyer/Client Relationships by Merit Bennet, J.D. Grounded in Jungian psychology, this book helps attorneys face their shadows and develop parts of mind and self that may be quashed in legal training (Santa Fe: The Message Company, 1997).

Law Practice Management Magazine. October 1999 issue on the theme of "A New Viewpoint: Redefining Lawyers' Work," includes "Time-Out Practice: Renewing Your Spirit, Reclaiming Your Life" by Steven Keeva; "Twelve Steps: Toward Personal Fulfillment in Law Practice" by Carl Horn; "Helping Clients Heal: Lessons Lawyers Can Teach Clients about Spiritual Growth" by Daniel Evans; and "Resolutionary View: 10 Principles for Developing the Attitude of Resolution." by Stewart Levine.

Leadership and the New Science. Learning about organizations from an orderly universe by Margaret J. Wheatley. This revolutionary and often poetic book uses lessons from "new science" to help people deal with troubling organizational issues including order and change, autonomy and control, structure and flexibility, planning and innovation (San Francisco: Berrett-Koehler, 1992).

Leading with the Wisdom of Love: Uncovering Virtue in People and Organizations by Dorothy Marcic. An inspiring call to incorporate the world's spiritual values into work based on research and experience. Marvelous exhibits (San Francisco: Jossey-Bass, 1997).

The Living Organization: Spirituality in the Workplace by William Guillory, the president and CEO of a human resource development firm and research scientist who is well-grounded in organizational development trends as well as his own personal spiritual journey (Salt Lake City: Innovations International, 1997).

Living with Vision: Reclaiming the Power of the Heart by Linda Marks. How to develop the capacity to see more clearly from the heart and soul, then create from your deepest values (Indianapolis: Knowledge Systems, 1991).

Opening the Mind's Eye: How Learning to Think outside the box Can Improve Any Practice by Steven Keeva. Outstanding article from the June 1996 *ABA Journal* on how lawyers need to and are becoming more creative. Available online through the articles section of www.transformingpractices.com.

Quest: A Guide for Creating Your Own Vision Quest by Denise Linn. A good overview of various quest traditions (including pilgrimages), then practical suggestions for designing a personal vision quest and integrating the wisdom of the quest into life and work (New York: Ballentine Books, 1997).

Renaissance Lawyer Society (www.renaissancelawyer.com). The central clearinghouse for information and links on major legal transformative movements. Extensive collection of articles; special interest groups on spirituality and law and various work-life excellence topics.

Sell Yourself without Selling Your Soul by Susan Harrow. A much-needed manual for anyone who needs to promote a business or a cause. Wise stories and tips melt the fear that promotion is inherently sleazy; model press releases and other products demonstrate how to gain attention with integrity (New York: Harper Collins, 2002).

Spirited Leading and Learning: Process Wisdom for a New Age by Peter B. Vaill. Essays by one of the movement's earliest and most respected leaders. Includes selections on leadership as a spiritual practice, the inherent spirit of organizations, and how to maintain spiritual values in turbulent times (San Francisco: Jossey-Bass, 1998).

Visionary Leadership by Burt Manus. Practical how-to guide for visionary leaders, with insights on the nature of vision, how to develop a vision, and how to implement it (San Francisco: Jossey Bass, 1992).

Notes

Introduction
Exploring a New World of Spirit at Work

1. Matthew Fox. *The Reinvention of Work* (Harper San Francisco, 1994).
2. Personal interview, summer 1999.
3. After the *Examiner* bought the *Chronicle* and sold its own name to another company, the column appeared in the *Chronicle* alone.
4. Huston Smith. *The Illustrated World's Religions: A Guide to Our Wisdom Traditions* (San Francisco: Harper, 1994), an updated version of his best-selling *Religions of Man*, which was first published in 1958.
5. Available in the archives of www.spiritatwork.com.
6. See chapter 3 for details.
7. Whenever first names only are used, they are pseudonyms. Job titles and other details may be changed to protect privacy.
8. George Gallup, Jr., and Tim Jones. *The Next American Spirituality* (Colorado Springs, CO: Chariot Viktor, May 2000).
9. Source: prepublication e-mail from Jones to Sullivan.
10. In Britain, industrial chaplains are like organizational development and transformational specialists. They help organizations define and practice their mission and values, as well as counsel individuals within the organization. Welbourn will send a copy of his sabbatical report if you write him at david@dwelbourn.freeserve.co.uk.

11. Bell is a former Passionist priest who is now principal of Inukshuk Management Consulting in Yellowknife, Northwest Territories (Canada). He specializes in helping aboriginal tribes deal with governments and corporations. For a revised copy of this talk and other articles on work, write Bell at mikebell@theedge.ca.

12. Telephone interview, October 12, 2001.

13. Tim Jones. *Awake My Soul: Practical Spirituality for Busy People* (New York: Doubleday, 1999), p. 9.

14. See Chapter 10 for information about how to find these exercises.

Chapter One
Discovering New Possibilities
for Meaning and Joy at Work

1. Growing up, I understood this to imply that movement (progress) is good; staying still equals stagnation. In some studies, when Asians were asked to interpret this saying, a typical comment was, "If you move too fast, you gather no wisdom."

2. Victor Frankl. *Man's Search for Meaning*, (Washington Square Press, Simon & Schuster, 1963 edition), p. 176.

3. www.geocities.com/~webwinds/frankl/meaning.htm. The paper also studies interpretations of meaning by Erich Fromm, Abraham Maslow, Rollo May, Krishnamurti, Paul Tillich, and Abraham Heschel.

4. Ibid.

5. This popular children's story may derive from an oral tradition inspired by the story of the Good Samaritan in Luke 10:25–37.

6. This version comes from *Ordinary Graces: Christian Teachings on the Interior Life*, edited by Lorraine Kisly (Berkeley: Conari Press, 2001), p. 94. It is drawn from *The Kitchen Saint and the Heritage of Islam*, translated by Elmer H. Douglas (Allison Park, PA: Pickwick Publications, copyright 1989).

Chapter Two
Seeing Your Work as a Spiritual Journey

1. Telephone interview, November 3, 2001.
2. Telephone interview, November 28, 2001.
3. Elizabeth O'Connor. *The Eighth Day of Creation* (Waco, TX: Word Books, 1971), p. 17. Ms. O'Connor comes from the Church of the Savior in Washington, D.C., an ecumenical church whose members help one another discover and develop their gifts. Among the gifts the church has created are a prison ministry, healing services for the homeless, a coffee house, and the Dayspring Retreat Center.
4. The story of the Post-it Note™ has been told in many business books and talks. This re-telling draws from these sources as well as Fry's delightful article, "The Choir Singer's Bookmark," which was published in the January 1989 issue of *Guideposts Magazine*.
5. Op. cit., p. 59.
6. See Chapter 10 for further suggestions.
7. Telephone interviews, August 2001.
8. St. John of the Cross. "The Dark Night," in *Mystics, Masters, Saints and Sages* (Berkeley, CA: Conari Press, 2001), p, 64.
9. Found on his website, www.davidroche.com
10. Telephone interview, September 8, 2001.
11. Jeff Salz. *The Way of Adventure: Transforming Your Life with Spirit and Vision* (John Wiley & Sons, 2000), p. 23.

Chapter Three
Creating and Using a Workplace Altar

1. As a white youth growing up in a segregated society, I was deprived of knowing about Dr. Bethune until the day I walked into the offices of the National Council of Negro Women (the founding of this organization was one of her many accomplishments) and was stunned by the dignity that radiated from her portrait. Rather than

give you a thumbnail sketch of her life, I urge you to research Dr. Bethune's story and let it inspire you as well. See e.g., www.vsca.sc.edu/aasc/bethune.htm).

Chapter Four
Turning Stress and Burnout into Energy and Insight

1. Capa specialized in photos showing the vitality of the human spirit in wartime or other difficult conditions. Excerpts from his autobiography, *Slightly Out of Focus*, can be found on www.amazon.com, and two new posthumous collections of his works were recently published. It's well worth a trip to the library to view some of the works of this master.
2. Personal interview, September 25, 2001.
3. For a better understanding of pride, self-will, fear, and the damage in our lives created by the images they evoke, see Susan Thesenga's *The Undefended Self: Living the Pathwork of Spiritual Wholeness* (Madison, VA: Pathwork Press, 1994).
4. Personal interview, August 2001.
5. The term *white space* in publishing refers to the use of wide margins or spacing between lines that allows the reader to avoid being overwhelmed with information. White space also provides orientation and direction by highlighting important points so they stand out from supporting information.
6. For more about contemplative practices, see the remaining chapters in this book.
7. Personal interview, September 25, 2001.
8. Personal interview, September 2001.

Chapter Five
Finding Wisdom for Work from Many Traditions

1. She must have been referring to rosary beads, which many Catholics use while praying. Prayer beads are

found in many traditions. Like Grandmother's crochet, prayer beads bring the hands (and by extension, the whole body) into the rhythm of prayer.

2. This term was apparently invented by Norman Lear, who used it in a speech to the members of the Washington Press Corps sometime in the early nineties.
3. Personal interview, January 10, 2001.
4. Richard Cimino and Don Lattin. *Shopping for Faith: American Religion in the New Millennium* (San Francisco: Jossey-Bass, 1998), p. 26.
5. Ibid., pp. 71–75.
6. www.religious tolerance.org/Hinduism.htm
7. Ibid.
8. "Sacred Texts: Hinduism" at www.sacredtexts.com/hin
9. *A Sourcebook for Earth's Community of Religions,* edited by Joel Beversluis (Grand Rapids: CoNexus Press, 1995).
10. Huston Smith. *The Illustrated World's Religions* (Harper San Francisco, 1994), p. 18–19.
11. Telephone interview, spring 1999.
12. This book is out of print.
13. Telephone interview, October 9, 2001.
14. Personal and telephone conversations, August–September 2001.
15. Personal interview, summer 1999.
16. Personal interview, summer 1999.
17. Personal interview, August 1998.
18. Cited in *Fast Company*, "Designing a Classroom that Works" by Maryann Hedaa at www.fastcompany.com/learning/braintrust/cdouglas.html.
19. For the complete article, see *Conscious Choice*, September 1996, available at www.consciouschoice.com/issues/cc095/rightlivelihood.html.
20. From "Are You Holding You Back" by Sandy Boucher in the April 1995 *Writer's Digest*. For the entire text, which is applicable to the creative process in every profession, see Boucher's website, www.sandyboucher.co.

21. "Clearness Committees and Their Use in Personal Discernment Notes" by Jan Hoffman, at www.nyym.org/leadings/clearness_hoffman.html.
22. Roberts's other inspirations were: 1) St. Francis of Assisi for his creativity, his ability to build effective teams, and his commitment to be an instrument of God's peace; 2) Howard Thurman, a little known African American who inspired Martin Luther King, Jr., and other civil rights leaders, and who led the cross-cultural Church for the Fellowship of All Peoples, in San Francisco; and 3) Abraham Heschel, a Jewish leader who escaped Nazi Germany and was instrumental in Christian-Jewish relations, including an involvement with the Second Vatican Council in the mid sixties.
23. Telephone interview, December 7, 2001.
24. Telephone interview, August 2001.

Chapter Six
Tapping Your Own Wisdom throughout the Workday

1. Telephone interview, 1999, while he was a doctoral student at the University of New Haven.
2. Summary of comments from various conversations, July–October 2001.
3. *Discalced* means shoeless. One of the reforms that St. John of the Cross and Teresa of Avila implemented in the order they co-founded was a return to simplicity. Hence, sandals, not shoes.
4. From the homepage of the Order of Carmelites (OCarm.), www.carmelites.com.
5. Telephone conversation, October 5, 2001.
6. Whether Dad created this affirmation or was quoting someone, I do not know.
7. Telephone interview, spring 1999.
8. The citation for the study was lost long ago. However, workshop participants have many times agreed with its findings.

9. Spiritual direction, as Jeffrey S. Gaines, M.Div., explains at www.sdiworld.org, is the "art of Christian listening carried out in the context of a one-to-one trusting relationship [in which trained guides 'companion'] another person, listening to that person's life story with an ear for the movement of the Divine." The process can be adapted to other faith traditions.

10. From the organization's homepage at www.hightor.org.

11. In an article at www.contemplativeoutreach.org.

12. This framing of Ignatian questions comes from Whitney Roberson, an Episcopal priest. For further information, see your local Jesuit community or search the web using the key words "Ignatian exercises." Several sites offer the complete exercises.

13. "Don't Burn Out!" *Fast Company*, May 2000, available on line at www.fastcompany.com/online/ 34/one.html.

14. See www.Taize.org for information.

Chapter Seven
Working with Integrity as Your Bottom Line

1. "What I Believe" by Albert Einstein, in *Out of My Latter Years* (London: Thomas & Hudson, 1950), p. 123.

2. The following meditation is adapted from the May 4, 2000, issue of the "Everyday Visionary Newsletter," which is available free from the author's website at www.visionary-resources.com.

3. Telephone conversation, early May 2002.

4. "The Emperor's New Clothes" by Hans Christian Andersen. The full text of the fable, as edited by Gerard Martin, can be found at www.geocities.com/athens/2424/clothes.html.

5. www.workforce.com/cgi-bin/iu.pl.

6. Both titles are available from Berret-Koehler publishers.

Chapter Eight
Creating Spiritual Community at and for Your Work

1. This quote from the movie script was found on the delightful website, www.filmsite.org, which features summaries and quotes from many film classics.
2. See www.ssnd.org for further information.
3. For information on this exquisitely researched handbook, see www.spiritualityatwork.com
4. For a copy of guidelines and resources, see www.bizstorytellers.org
5. Personal interviews, August 2001.
6. fastcompany.com/online/34/one.html.
7. Personal interview, summer 1999.
8. See www.thepresidiodialogues.org.
9. For tips on starting a SIG on spirit and work, contact dfleck@itswithin.com.

Chapter Nine
Envisioning and Re-Visioning
Your Work and Your Profession

1. From *Out of My Life and Thought* by Albert Schweitzer, as cited in *Albert Schweitzer: An Anthology*, edited by Charles R. Joy (Beacon Press, 1947), p. 259.
2. Frederick Franck. *The Zen of Seeing: Seeing and Drawing as Meditation* (New York: Vintage Books, 1973). This recently re-issued book is one of twenty-eight by Franck, who is still creating and loving in his nineties.
3. *The Schweitzer Album: A Portrait in Words and Pictures by Erica Anderson, with Additional Text by Albert Schweitzer* (New York: Harper & Row, 1965, p. 26).
4. To reclaim the power of wishful thinking, imitate four-year-olds, who spout possibilities with exuberance, gusto, and an utter lack of justification for why they want something one moment and something totally different the next. Then develop adult brainstorming

skills and learn to anchor your imagination in your heart, not in your projections on others. "I want my boss to change," for instance, is generally as unproductive a wish as "I want my husband (wife) to change." "I want a fulfilling and ethical relationship with my boss," however, opens the door to many possibilities, including: 1) seeing new dimensions in your current relationship; 2) the possibility that you are called to another job; and/or 3) opening dialogues and finding allies that help you and your boss to create a more ethical and fulfilling relationship.

5. Business plan outlines and information are available also at www.sba.gov
6. Walter Brueggemann. *Prophetic Imagination* (Fortress Press, June 2001).
7. Telephone conversation, October 2001.
8. Telephone conversation, November 2001.
9. This traditional Mexican holiday honors death as a liberation of the spirit. After ancestral graves are cleaned and decorated, families may picnic on them while sharing stories of the ancestors. Candies and artwork show the intermingling of death and life, thus helping to break the fear of death.

Chapter Ten
Resources for Meaningful and Satisfying Work

1. For leadership resources, see www.spiritatwork.com, www.mgeneral.com, or the bibliography to David Welbourn's sabbatical report ("A Spiritual Pilgrimage to Corporate America: A Report of a Sabbatical Study on Spirituality and Business Organisations" by British Industrial chaplain David Welbourn).

Acknowledgments

Thanking all the people whose meaningful and joyous work has led to this book would fill another book. Thus, formal acknowledgment is given here only to those whose encouragement and assistance led directly to this book, which was conceived over breakfast with Al Gustafson at MacDonald's Hamburger University in February 2001. Our meeting stemmed from (1) an invitation from Stewart Levine to participate in the American Bar Association's Future Search Process for its Law Practice Management Section and (2) sharing with Al some of the columns on spirit and work that I wrote from 1999 to 2001, first for the *San Francisco Examiner* and then the *San Francisco Chronicle*.

Thank you, Stewart, for many years of sharing vision, values, and friendship. Thank you Dave Murphy of the *San Francisco Chronicle*, for making room in the paper for approximately twenty-six "Vision and Values" columns. Thank you, Al, for connecting me with Jeremy Langford of Sheed & Ward. Thank you, Jeremy and Managing Editor Kass Dotterweich, for good, tough editing.

Thank you, clients, who have taught me how to work with vision and spirit in challenging situations. Thank you, interviewees, who enriched the columns and this book with your inspiration and insights. Thank you, Rhena Schweitzer Miller, for stories about how to be one's own person in relationship to a parent with a powerful presence. They came just when I needed them.

Thank you, Matthew Fox, for books that brought my husband John and me from Washington, D.C., to Oakland, California. Thank you, Judi Neal and Martin Rutte, for several years of encouragement to write about spirit and work. Thank you, Sherry Connelly, for creating wonderful ways that people can meet to discuss spirit and work. Thank you, colleagues in the field of spirit and work who have helped shape ideas, particularly Chuck Burack, Elizabeth Doty, Diane Fleck, Deborah Frangquist, John Renesch, Whitney Roberson, Roseanne Roberts, and Suzanne Zeman. Thank you, Kim Wright, founder of Renaissance Lawyer Society, and fellow board members Donna Boris, Dolly Garlo, Kevin Ginzberg, Carolyn Hansen, Maureen Holland, Neil Olsen, Cheryl Stephens, Allison Tiffany, Jennifer Tull, and Marilyn Westerfield for the opportunity to help bring spirit and vision to the legal profession. Thank you, Steven Keeva of the *Journal of the American Bar Association* for the connection to Kim, for enlivening and often funny conversations, and for setting the standard for a book that applies spiritual principles to professional work. Thank you, Phyllis Weiss Hesserot, of the Interest Group on Worklife Excellence, for your ongoing support and encouragement.

Thank you to fellow members of our twelve-year writing group—Anne Hillman, Carole Peccorini, and Harriet Wright—and to longtime writer friends Roy Aarons, Donna Reifsnider, and Lauren DeBoer. Thank you to friends and family who have encouraged my writing, especially Joshu Boneh, Kari Kashani, Aunt Bunny Millsaps, cousins Janice Kitner and Andrea Lee, and my mother-in-law, Ruth Sullivan. Thank you to my brother Bill McHenry for your straight-forward viewpoint and ability to share just the right few words when they are most needed.

Thank you to everyone who is helping me learn how to market a book. Thanks especially to Nathan Bubenzer, who began the process of marketing at Sheed & Ward, and to Kanishka Gangopadhyay, who is completing it. Thank you, Susan Harrow, for your guidance on how to transform media shyness to media nerviness. Thank you, Kantryn Hall, for helping to demystify the process of promotion, and to

Randy Haykin, for many new ideas and insights into how the book may be useful in faith communities.

Special thanks go to the memory of Sue Drobbin and Billie Smith. For almost all my life, Billie was another mother, confidante, role model, and mentor. Sue was a creative model, a loving friend for more than a quarter of a century, bridesmaid, repository of jokes, and connector to common friends. The passage of Sue and Billie during the writing of this book was devastating; the encouragement of their spirits is always present.

And then there are the two people without whom this work would just not have been possible. My sister Peggy Printz and my husband John Sullivan have been my major cheerleaders, research associates, posers of questions, listeners of frustration, deflators of ego, anchors of faith. John has also been chief tender of cats, housekeeper, and primary wage earner during the months that writing this book took over my life. Thank you both.